SWEETER THAN HONEY

▉ Foundations series

Testifying to the faith and creativity of the Orthodox Christian
Church, the Foundations series draws upon the riches of its
tradition to address the modern world. These survey texts are
suitable both for preliminary inquiry and deeper investigation,
in the classroom or for personal study.

Peter C. Bouteneff
Series Editor

BOOK 1
Stages on Life's Way: Orthodox Thinking on Bioethics
by John and Lyn Breck

BOOK 2
Seeds of the Word: Orthodox Thinking on Other Religions
by John Garvey

BOOK 3
Sweeter Than Honey: Orthodox Thinking on Dogma and Truth
by Peter C. Bouteneff

BOOK 3 OF THE FOUNDATIONS SERIES

Sweeter Than Honey

ORTHODOX THINKING
ON DOGMA AND TRUTH

Peter C. Bouteneff

ST VLADIMIR'S SEMINARY PRESS
CRESTWOOD, NEW YORK
2006

Library of Congress Cataloging-in-Publication Data

Bouteneff, Peter.
    Sweeter than honey : Orthodox thinking on dogma and truth / by Peter C.
Bouteneff.
        p.   cm.   — (Foundations series, bk. 3)
    Includes bibliographical references.
    ISBN–13: 978–0–88141–307–6 (alk. paper)
    ISBN–10: 0–88141–307–0 (alk. paper)
    1. Orthodox Eastern Church—Doctrines.   2. Truth—Religious aspects—
Christianity.   I. Title.   II. Series: Foundations series (St. Vladimir's Orthodox
Theological Seminary (Crestwood, Tuckahoe, Westchester County, N.Y.)); bk. 3.

BX320.3.B68   2006
230'.19—dc22

                                                            2006012937

© 2006 BY PETER C. BOUTENEFF

ST VLADIMIR'S SEMINARY PRESS
575 Scarsdale Rd, Crestwood, NY 10707
1–800–204–2665
www.svspress.com

ISSN 1556–9837
ISBN 0–88141–307–0
ISBN 978–0–88141–307–6

PRINTED IN THE UNITED STATES OF AMERICA

For Vera Bouteneff

CONTENTS

The ordinances of the Lord are true,
and righteous altogether.
More to be desired are they than gold,
even much fine gold;
sweeter also than honey,
and drippings of the honeycomb.
—Psalm 19.9–10

introduction

Orthodox Christianity makes a stunning claim: the teachings found in Scripture interpreted within the community of the Church are true. What's more, they are not merely true for the community that produces and receives them but simply *true*. They describe the way things really are.

In our age, several factors challenge anyone's ability to make claims about truth.

Religious pluralism is a challenge. Many faith traditions claim to be teaching the truth but are apt to come to opposing conclusions. Any person aware of the surrounding world is struck by the fact that people of wisdom and goodwill often believe and teach radically different things about life and its meaning. Many conclude that no single religious teaching could possibly claim to be *the* truth, particularly if that means saying that some teachings or some people are wrong.

Postmodernism is a challenge. The intellectual climate current in universities works on the principles that no teaching can claim absolute value and that no text can claim absolute authority. This stems partly from the conviction that words—our only hold on reality—have no fixed meaning. More broadly, in the media and in popular culture, people's good intentions to respect one another's beliefs and lifestyles often turn into moral and intellectual relativism.

Fundamentalism is a challenge. In reaction to pluralism and post-modern relativism, some people have tended to build walls thicker and higher, to establish religious and cultural identities in opposition to others, and to back them up with violence, whether doctrinal or physical. The fanatical approach to absolute truth, which we witness in a particularly sharp way today, leads many to swear off convictions altogether.

In short, our prevailing culture dictates that it is impossible to assert that any one thing is true for everyone. Which means that it is impossible to say that one thing is true and therefore another false.

An Orthodox Christian is left in a quandary:

* How do I dare claim that my faith community speaks the truth when so many other reasonable and wise people claim otherwise?

* How do I dare claim, without being a fanatic, that my community's teachings are true in some way for everyone?

* How do I dare even converse about truth when our words—particularly words like God or salvation—can take on such vastly different meanings?

The first portion of this book is concerned with answering these questions, viewing them through the lens of Orthodox Christian teaching.

The study and meaning of truth is a rich subject that has received serious treatment at the hands of philosophers, theologians, scientists, and poets. This book doesn't aim to cover the subjects of truth and epistemology (the study of knowing) in any exhaustive way. Its aims are to establish the viability of believing that something is true at all, and the viability of believing that it is true universally.

These aims demand exploration of several areas: the nature of truth, objectivity, and subjectivity, the nature of language—religious language in particular, as well as the nature of story and myth. In that inquiry I will draw on some ancient and modern sources. I will also seek to give credible sense to the ideas of dogma and authority, words with especially negative connotations in our day.

Dogma and Truth

If the first half of the book is concerned with establishing the existence of truth and grounding it in the person of Jesus Christ, the second seeks to build on that foundation by exploring how the Orthodox Church discerns and formulates its teachings. How does the Church arrive at conclusions that it considers the truth about God and the world? Here, too, there are several challenges.

Expressing concepts that are ultimately unknowable and unprovable is a challenge. We claim to say meaningful, even binding, things about God, but how do we square this claim with the fact that God is unknowable and beyond human expression? Doesn't God's ultimate unknowability make it impossible to make assured statements about him?

Identifying the sources and expressions of truth is a challenge. From where do we derive our beliefs and teachings about God and the world? An informed observation of the natural world can lead us to good conclusions about the relationships we have with God, with each other, and with the natural environment. But what informs that observation? What are the texts, rites, and symbols that we consider truth-bearing, and why do we give them priority over other sources?

Correctly understanding these sources of truth is a challenge. It's not enough to identify these sources. We have to decide who understands them correctly and why. The Bible is not self-interpreting; the same Bible leads different people to radically different conclusions. How do we read and understand it and the other sources of our theology?

The second part of this book is therefore concerned with how the Orthodox Church arrives at the teachings it considers true. We will investigate written, oral, visual, and ritual sources and expressions of theology and will discover how these sources allow us to reach conclusions about God and the world.

Orthodox Christian Particularity

I have written this book for Orthodox Christians seeking to make their faith more real and engaged, as well as for anyone wondering how an Orthodox Christian might think about truth and dogma.

I also have written from an explicitly Christian point of view. In reference to truth, I take Jesus Christ to be "the way, the truth, and the life" (Jn 14.6). But what makes this book *Orthodox* Christian? How exclusive is its approach?

Orthodox Christians aren't the only ones to claim that there is such a thing as absolute truth, nor are we the only people to claim that what we believe is true, and true universally. Virtually all sources of theology cited in this book are shared, to different extents, among all Christians. The Orthodox have no exclusive claim to the Bible; nearly all Christians share our claim that it is the preeminent written revelation of God about himself and his relationship to this world. We are also hardly the only ones to be interested in the writings of the Church Fathers and the pronouncements of the ecumenical councils, although the authority we give them does distinguish us from a sizeable contingent of the Christian world. Even Christians who do not depend on other ancient sources come to some of the same basic conclusions as the Orthodox, that Jesus Christ is the Son of God—the Savior of the world.

If this book finds resonance across confessional lines, and if much is in agreement with philosophy, sociology, science, and people's empirical conclusions, that is a good thing. It should come as no surprise that human beings created in God's image read the world in which God reveals himself and come to similar conclusions.

There will doubtless be points where Orthodox uniquenesses will appear. There is a particular character to our synthesis of Scripture, patristic writing, conciliar formulations—especially our liturgical texts and iconography—and to the ways in which these sources collectively generate our theological thought and teaching. Unsurprising, really, given the different lines along which Eastern and Western Christian thought and culture have traveled, especially in the second millennium of Christian history.

This book is also about the value of dialogue, of agreement and disagreement. One of my main theses is that true knowledge and genuine communication are possible. Once upon a time, this was not such a radical claim. But it means that real agreement and real disagreement are also possible. Where we disagree, therefore, let us engage our differences and take them seriously, since some of our divergences can be about matters of life and death. Dogma and truth, sweeter than honey, are such matters.

If we are honest with each other, both our convergences and our divergences can lead to profound reflection within our faith communities and in ourselves. They will lead to real, respectful, and possibly transformative encounters. But let it all be based on the agreed-on understanding that there is such a thing as truth, and that it can be known.

Finally, as a part of the Foundations series, this book is intended for a broad audience: it is a survey text for preliminary inquiry as well as deeper investigation. Many of the topics treated here, especially in part one, are difficult to write about simply. My hope is that beginning inquirers will feel drawn in, even as more experienced readers will feel that I have at least represented the complexity of the issues involved. I fear that I will disappoint both, by being at the same time needlessly complex and too lightweight. If this book works at all, it is in large part owing to the comments and advice of several readers, notably Fr Thomas Hopko, Fr John McGuckin, Fr John Breck, Fr John Behr, and Dr Patricia Fann Bouteneff, as well as to the ideas I've garnered from many other friends, students, and partners in conversation.

part one

DOGMA AND TRUTH

chapter one

DOGMA AND TRUTH: FIRST THOUGHTS ON KNOWING

I n most Western societies today, dogma does not leap out as an attractive concept. A good way to alienate an audience is to tell them that you are talking about dogma or that you want to be dogmatic about something. They will tune out: dogma conjures images of arbitrary authority, of fixed rules that fly in the face of evidence. There is no need to prove dogmas; you believe them because they're dogmas. Dogmatic pronouncements emanate from unbending and uncreative minds; they rule out discussion, reflection, and interpretation.

This is not a pretty picture. If the word dogma is to be used credibly, it needs rescuing. The ideas behind the word need to be revived and explored: the ideas that there is such a thing as absolute truth about God and the world, that this truth can be discerned, that it can be an object of faith and love, that it is the root of creativity and freedom.

Christian dogma, for the believer, is linked with truth. It has to be, otherwise our adherence to dogma is groundless, not to say pointless. If dogma has no serious basis in the truth, then our membership in the Church and our struggle with the beliefs taught there are no more meaningful than membership in a fraternity or club.

It would seem obvious to state that we believe dogma to be true, yet it's not obvious at all. A great many people both within and outside the Church see dogma simply as rules made up by people throughout history. Made up not just by people but by an all-male, conservative cabal out of touch with today's realities. Others may be less suspicious of the process by which dogma was generated but don't see any particular need to involve themselves with the teachings of the Church. These might see the Church chiefly in social terms, as a pretext for fellowship with people of like mind or ethnic heritage. Or they might concede that, although dogma lends coherence to the whole enterprise that is the Church, it is a necessary evil, best left to the experts and enthusiasts. Some insist that dogma gets in the way of their relationship with Jesus.

Taking dogma as truth, then, can be challenging. When we believe dogmas, not just because they're dogmas but because we consider them to be actually true, conveying the truth about the world, about its Creator, about humanity and its situation, the results can be revolutionary. At that point, we realize that we had better come to know these teachings and take them seriously. If they really do convey the truth about life, we want to seek it, and seek to understand it.

In seeking the truth, however, we need to be prepared for revolution, and this can be frightening. Once we start to wrestle with the teachings of the Church as if they are absolutely true, we realize that we might have to change. We might have to rethink our lives, behave differently, reason about the world differently. Change might be uncomfortable, but consider it we must, because otherwise we may be in denial about reality.

And yet, the liturgy of the Church reveals a craving to know the truth, God's truth. At Matins and at Vespers—the morning and evening prayers of the Church—we sing the verses from Psalm 119, "Blessed are you, O Lord, teach me your statutes! . . . enlighten me with your precepts!" So we regularly beg God to help us to know and understand his statutes, his commandments, his precepts—because these are the grounding of the world that he created. We want to be coming to know and comprehend the truth, and to live by it. That's how we understand dogma. It is true.

Now, what about truth?

What Is Truth?

Just about everyone is for truth, just as everyone is for love or beauty. But to quote Pontius Pilate, "What is truth?" The dictionary tells us, not very helpfully, that truth is that which is true. Truth is the reality underlying appearances. We could simply say that something is true when it conforms to genuine, existing reality.

Truth as Relation, Truth as Action

Seeing truth as "fact" is a start. But to get to the truth about truth, we have to see it as far more than sheer fact or accuracy. When John Keats said that beauty is truth, and truth beauty, he was onto something. He was linking truth with something beyond just the veracity of things; in his case specifically with aesthetic experience, something we feel and perceive, engage with, something that is beautiful, good. There is a great deal to be said about the relationship between truth and beauty.[1] But for now I want to highlight just one point:

Truth is something you enter into a relationship with.

Taking cues from the Scriptures, the Christian goes still further. Truth is linked to a way of life, one that is in concert with the way things really are. Truth is not just something that we learn; it is something that we do, how we live. Truth can be an action, an activity. St Paul writes in Ephesians 4.15 about "speaking the truth in love," or at least that's how it's commonly translated. The Greek here uses truth as a verb—*aletheuo*—so that Paul is really talking about "truthing" in love. That means speaking, thinking, and acting rightly, truly, honestly—and with love, lest we forget the *relational* dimension of truth.

The Scriptures speak in the same breath about walking before God "in truth, with a true heart" and doing "that which is pleasing in the sight of God."[2] Isaiah 26.10 talks about *learning* righteousness and *doing* the truth.[3] We usually think of it the other way around, doing righteousness and learning the truth. But the two are related. Knowing the truth and living the truth are two sides of the same coin, because, as St John Chrysostom said, "Virtue is really true; vice is falsehood."[4] Or as we have it from

---

[1]See, for example, David Bentley Hart, *The Beauty of the Infinite: The Aesthetics of Christian Truth* (Grand Rapids, MI: Eerdmans, 2003).

[2]See, for example, 1 Kg 2.4; 2 Kg 20.3; Is 38.3.

[3]The scriptural verses cited here are taken from the Septuagint (LXX).

[4]*Homilies on the Epistle of St Paul to the Philippians*, hom. 14.

1 John 2.4, "He who says 'I know him [Jesus Christ]' but disobeys his commandments is a liar, and the truth is not in him."

Truth entails action, and knowing-doing the truth is the substance of salvation. St Paul writes that God "desires that everyone be saved and come to knowledge of the truth" (1 Tim 2.4). To be saved is to know the truth about things. And to know the truth about things is both grounding and liberating; in Jesus' words, "You shall know the truth, and the truth shall set you free" (Jn 8.32).

But the context of this saying is revealing: "*If you remain in my word*, you are truly my disciples, and you will know the truth, and the truth will make you free." He links "knowing the truth" with "being in his word" or, in Greek, his *logos*. Remaining in the word or *logos* of Jesus means to be "in the sense of Jesus;" it means being true to who he is and what he does. If we think-speak-act in accordance with Christ, only then will we know the truth, and be set free.

But Jesus goes one step further when says to his disciples, "I am the way, the truth, and the life" (Jn 14.6). What could he mean? He could mean simply that he speaks the truth and is trustworthy. Some say that this pronouncement shows Jesus in an unattractive light: he sounds so full of himself! And he excludes other expressions of truth. But a genuine follower of Jesus Christ interprets these words only in their fullest sense, to refer to absolute truth itself: Jesus links truth not only with salvation, freedom, and action but also with his own person. This is remarkable, to be sure. But Christians can believe no less.

Who Is Truth? Truth as Person

If we take Jesus' words seriously, one of the conclusions we reach is that truth is personal. Of course, if you just say that truth is personal, it sounds as if you are saying that it is relative, that it varies from person to person. In this case, however, we mean that truth is *identified with a person.*

How does this work itself out?

I'm going to get a bit technical here. To begin with, let's stay within St John's gospel, a book that has a great deal to say about Jesus and the truth. This gospel begins by identifying Jesus Christ with the Word (Logos) of God. The first three verses speak of the Word of God, who is in the beginning with God, who *is* God (i.e., divine). This Word-Logos is the perfect expression of who and what God is, the one through whom the universe is created, the Logos underlying the logic of everything that is.[5]

Jesus Christ, the one born of Mary, is this Word-Logos of God, also known as the Son of God. When Mary gave birth to Jesus, no new person came into existence; rather, the Word himself became flesh (Jn 1.14). As we sing during the Christmas feast, the one who exists as divine from before all the ages is now born as a babe. He is beyond time, beyond history, but he enters history at a particular time and place:

> Today, he who holds creation in the hollow of his hand
>   is born of a Virgin.
> He who in his essence cannot be handled is wrapped in
>   swaddling clothes.

[5]See Heb 1.2–3; Col 1.17.

God lies in a manger, the one who created the heavens in the beginning!

That is who Christ is—the one who established the world, the very one whom the ancient Greek poets had in mind in speaking of the one "in whom we live, and move, and have our being" (see Acts 17.28). He is the one "in whom all things hold together" (Col 1.17), the one who gives integrity to every existing thing. This is why John, again, writes that grace and truth come through Jesus Christ (Jn 1.17). Christ doesn't just speak the truth, he *is* the truth.

All of this means that if we are seeking the truth of the world, the reason, logic, and integrity that underlie the world, we are in fact seeking the one in whom all things hold together, the one in whom we live and move and have our existence, the one by whom the universe came to be—Jesus Christ.

Christ is the truth, but not in isolation from the Father and the Spirit. We understand God as the one who exists eternally with his Son and his Holy Spirit. When we associate truth with the person of Jesus, we aren't limiting that association to the Son alone. Truth, ultimately, is trinitarian. Truth is an attribute of God the Father himself. It is a characteristic that God possesses in his very nature; it is an aspect of what God is. Christ is "the Truth" as the Son and Word of the Father. He is the expression of God's own being, his perfect image (Col 1.15). He is the stamp or seal of the very person of God (Heb 1.3). So he is the truth, God's truth, God's wisdom.

Scripture also speaks of the Holy Spirit, the "Spirit of Truth" (Jn 14.17; 15.26). This Spirit, Jesus says, guides us into all truth.

How does the Spirit do this? By leading us to Jesus (Jn 16.13–14). St John even says that "the Spirit *is* the truth," in the sense that the Spirit is the witness to Jesus Christ (1 Jn 5.7). The Spirit of truth is the one who shows us who Jesus is—the Logos-Word and Son of God the Father. (We will say more about this in chapter 5.)

Truth therefore describes and is described by the three persons of the Trinity—Father, Son, and Holy Spirit. But Christ, the expressed Word of God who became human and lived among us, represents in his person the totality of God's revelation of truth.

Truth, in the New Testament, is identified with Jesus Christ, consistently and indisputably. What does this imply for human beings, whether or not they are Christian?

Jesus as the Universal Truth

Scripture identifies Jesus Christ not just with Christian truth, as opposed to everyone else's truth, but with universal truth, the truth for everyone and everything. Justin Martyr, the great second-century apologist, believed that the Logos (the Word, whom we know as Jesus Christ) is a "sowing Logos" (*Logos spermatikos*)—one who disseminates seeds. This is why we believe that truth, "seeds of the Word," are found in diverse faiths and systems of thought. Regardless of whether Jesus is named as such, and regardless of whether these belief systems came before or after the first-century life of Jesus of Nazareth, nevertheless Jesus—the Word of God—is there as the ground of whatever is true. That which is true within philosophy before and outside of Christianity is true because of "the seeds of the Word." In one of his more famous passages, Justin writes, "Whatever things were rightly said among all people are the property of us Christians. For next to God, we worship and love the Word who is from the unbegotten and ineffable God . . . [And] all the writers were able to see realities darkly through the sowing of the implanted word that was in them."[6]

According to this line of thinking, everything that is true, whether or not it is said by a Christian, is true because of Christ; anything that is approaching truth is approaching Christ. And everyone who is doing the truth is making some kind of approach to Christ, whether or not they name him as Christ. As Christ himself says, "Everyone who is of the truth hears my voice" (Jn 18.37).

Card-carrying, Bible-reading Christians do not hold a monopoly on truth. People of all backgrounds and faith traditions can and do come to right conclusions about created reality and about God himself. But where this happens, whether in the person of a Christian, Muslim, Jew, Hindu, or Buddhist, we point to Christ, and we locate the fulfillment of that truth in Christ. This is how we apply our belief that Christ is the way, the truth, and the life.

The universal application of this teaching has led some to speak of "implicit" or "anonymous" Christians.[7] The idea of "anonymous Christianity" suggests that when people believe things that are true and live in God's grace ("doing the truth"), even they if employ names and terminology that are not explicitly Christian, they draw nearer to Christ and are enlightened by Christ, "the true light who enlightens *every* human being" (Jn 1.9, my emphasis). This doesn't mean that everybody is a Christian, whether they

---

[6]*Second Apology*, 13.

[7]The latter expression is particularly associated with the twentieth-century Roman Catholic theologian Karl Rahner.

know it or not. It only means that when they are doing or believing the truth, they are drawing closer to Christ.

There is something attractive, inclusive, and inviting about this idea. While preserving the universality and uniqueness of the person of Christ, the idea of the anonymous Christian respects truth and goodness wherever it is found. It rings true, for looking through the right eyeglasses, we see profound and joyous convergences in the thought, teaching, and mystical experiences of the world's religious traditions. Some have attributed these convergences to a trait embedded in humanity—a collective subconscious that has evolved as a result of our "wiring." But what if these convergences exist because of a single, actual truth? What if that truth is the truth of Jesus Christ?

If there is a collective subconscious that points in the direction of a transcendent being, if there are teachings about avatars or incarnate divine beings, other "sons of God," if there are other myths about creation and fall, other myths about cataclysmic floods, other stories about virgin births, then all of these are like strings that resonate, sometimes more, sometimes less, with one grounding note, whom we believe to be none other than Jesus himself, the eternal Son of God, in whom all things hold together.

On the other hand, the category of anonymous Christian might sound patronizing: many Muslims, Hindus, Buddhists, or Jews might not enjoy being called anonymous Christians just because some of their views happen to square with our own. "Let me be a Muslim, because that's what I am, and not an 'anonymous Christian'!" It would be especially offensive to give the sense that non-Christians merit the title of "anonymous Christians" only in those instances when they've hit the truth, and then go back to being what they were all the rest of the time. The category has obvious limitations.

Yet I wonder: when a devout practitioner of Islam calls me an anonymous Muslim based on what I believe and how I live my life, I might well be glad.[8] At least I would know that I am talking with someone who takes his or her faith as true. Our dialogue could then proceed on a vital foundation: the common conviction that there is an absolute truth and that our faith has universal significance.

Types of Truth

We are still left with the question of how the formula "Jesus Christ = *the* truth" works itself out in day-to-day life and thought, in our interaction with truth. Obviously we can't substitute *Jesus Christ* for the word *truth* whenever it comes up in our discourse. Part of it is a language problem: the word truth is used in different contexts and on different levels, which don't always relate perfectly to one another. There are different kinds of things about which we might want to know the truth. On the scientific level, we might want to know the truth about the nature of antimatter, supernovas, or quarks. On the circumstantial level, we might want to know the truth about who really killed JFK or about where we left our keys this morning. On the theological level, we may want to know the truth about how the Father, the Son, and the Holy Spirit count as one God. Then there is also the

---

[8]Such formulations, or their spirit, are present in some Muslim reflections on Christianity. See, for example, Seyyed Hossein Nasr, "The Islamic View of Christianity," in *Christianity among World Religions,* eds. Hans Küng and Jürgen Moltmann (Edinburgh: T&T Clark, 1986), 3–12.

truth about the *meaning* of things: among others, what is the meaning of the AIDS pandemic, and why does God allow so many to suffer and die in this way?

These are different kinds of questions, and they would almost seem to require different definitions of truth. Some questions have a simple yes or no answer: Are you in the kitchen? Other questions have multiple correct answers or admit a variety of approaches that are more or less apt: Why does God allow suffering? There are still other questions for which there might not even be a true answer—in other words, false questions: Is this room purple or black? (when the room is in fact painted white). Truth doesn't even need to be an answer to a question. With no claims to be making an exhaustive account of the philosophy of truth, I would like to explore and evaluate one common paradigm of truth.

Verifiability

Adherents of the philosophy of logical positivism reckon truth by means of two different categories:

1. *Things that are verifiable as true or false.* For example, to say that the earth is roughly spherical is verifiably true. To say that the tree outside my window is made of stone is verifiably false. Many of these things we take on trust and don't bother verifying—such as, gravity will pull airborne objects toward the ground—but they are verifiable nonetheless.

2. *Things that are not verifiable as true or false.* These are things that are believed to be true or false but cannot be proved to be so. For example, to say that there is a

personal being outside the universe who created the universe is widely believed to be true but is not verifiable through any irrefutable external evidence.

It makes a certain sense to say that if you can't prove that something is true or false, then your statement has limited meaning. I can say, "Aliens from a UFO descended to earth and performed a medical examination on me," but unless I can prove that it happened (or unless someone can prove that it didn't), my assertion will draw more attention to my mental health than to supposed extraterrestrial visitations.

But limiting truth to these two categories—verifiable and not—leaves out a great deal. First, they don't do justice to the truth of stories. Stories about things that didn't necessarily happen historically as written can be true, and they stand outside of the clean categories of verifiability. The truth of Jonah's odyssey (with the whale, the plant, and the worm) is not dependent on its status as a historical event, nor is it intended to be. (More on this in chapter 3.)

Depending entirely on verifiability leaves too many things out of the picture: there are scientific theories (such as string theory) that are not verifiable, but nonetheless useful. It also leaves God out of the picture. There is no external, incontrovertible proof of the existence of God. More importantly, the logic of verifiability makes God into just another object that can be believed to exist or not to exist, on a par with created things like trees and people. But God, in proper religious thinking, is radically other than any existing thing. God is not another thing but the foundation of everything, the light of everything, the life of everything. It's like C. S. Lewis writes in *The Weight of Glory*: "I believe in

Christianity as I believe the sun has risen, not only because I see it but because by it I see everything else."

Finally, although the verifiability of statements about physical reality and spiritual reality may reside on different levels, it would be wrong to suggest that spiritual reality resides solely on the level of unverifiable faith. There are well-established conditions for verifiability in the scientific realm: for example, the person testing an assertion has to be of a sound mind and basing his or her assertion on other verifiable evidence. There are similar conditions for the verifiability and knowledge of spiritual truth: the consistent claim of Christian tradition is that if one leads a right, moral life, seeks truth, and prays, then he or she will come to knowledge of God—not just to a surmising about God, not to a tentative faith or a rational supposition about God. Through prayer, through renouncing immorality (by telling the truth, by checking one's lust for power, money, and sex, by treating others and the created world with love and kindness, and so on), the person will come to know, by immediate experience, the presence of God.

Jesus in the Types of Truth

Yet whatever we say about verifiability, we come back to the point that there are different ways to speak of things as true, that truth pertains to a wide variety of lines of inquiry and ways of speaking. Where is Jesus Christ in all of this? Where is he in the truth about quarks and supernovas, the truth about JFK, the truth of science and of stories, the truth about war, death, and AIDS?

Whenever, in any question or pursuit, one approaches verity, genuineness, reality, a right way, a true approach, or a true answer, one approaches Christ. Better put, wherever there is truth, genuineness, reality, it's because of Christ. This is why St Paul can write to the Philippians, "Whatever is true, whatever is honorable, whatever is just, whatever is pure, whatever is lovely, whatever is gracious, if there is any excellence, if there is anything worthy of praise, think about these things" (Phil 4.8). Because in thinking about these things, Paul says, our minds are on Jesus Christ. In the next chapter of the same letter he says, "Once you were darkness, but now you are light in the Lord; walk as children of light, for *the fruit of light is found in all that is good and right and true*" (Eph 5.8–9, emphasis added).

Conversely, anywhere there is deceit or distortion of truth; where there is a degree of denial on however deep a level; where we are dishonest—out of convenience or out of the need for power or gratification or out of misinformation or ignorance—or if we are "living a lie"; there is distance from Christ himself.

Furthermore, any philosophical, spiritual, or religious teaching, to the extent that it genuinely denies the identity of Christ as the divine Son through whom everything was created, is distanced from the truth. If closeness to truth means closeness to Christ, then leaving the truth means leaving Christ—and vice versa. Leave Christ and you are leaving the truth. You can still do good science; you can still be an outstandingly good person. But you won't know the truth about the universe and its Creator. Which means that you won't know the foundations of your science or of who you really are.

Truth as Subjectivity

Earlier, I said that the identification of truth with the person of Jesus Christ means that truth is not an abstract, impersonal category but is personal. This seems to contradict a basic intuition: we generally think of truth as impersonal and objective. Don't we come to know the truth about anything through detachment, through an objective gathering of evidence processed by reason? We are more likely to get to the bottom of things if we strip away emotional involvement. Emotional, personal engagement will only cloud our rational judgment.

That is certainly the logic of Western thought, especially as it developed after the Enlightenment. And it works. Observation benefits from the clarity of detachment. In science, detachment is often (though not always) a condition for coming to right conclusions. Practical experiments prove or disprove hypotheses. The resulting truth is objective; it doesn't depend on who perceives it. An acid combined with a base will produce a salt, every time. Of course, science is more complicated than that, and few scientists today believe in perfect objectivity as an attainable or even fully desirable starting point. Hypotheses are often arrived at through subjectivity, through intuition. And modern science, perhaps especially modern physics, has learned to account for a certain uncertainty, a predictable unpredictability.

Although the ideals of objectivity and reason have been increasingly brought into doubt, the scientific approach to truth can still be defined as an overwhelming tendency toward objective reasoning. Again, such an approach is enormously useful within much human inquiry, but it doesn't work for every kind of question. The attempt to be scientific within human pursuits of love and meaning, for example, is doomed to failure. The misguided professor who seeks the formula for love or for the soul is a classic subject of comedy, and sometimes tragedy. We rightly bring our powers of observation and reason to bear on such questions, but if we believe that perfect detachment will yield truth, we are mistaken.

In our time many scientists themselves have come to know that knowledge and understanding come with engagement and faith. Whereas Plato inscribed above the door of his academy, "Let no one enter who does not know geometry," physicist Max Planck had inscribed above the door to his laboratory, "Let no one enter here who does not have faith." As computer whiz Guy Kawasaki has said, "Some things need to be believed to be seen."

Once our understanding of truth is rounded out, going beyond the cold, observable facts to their underlying meaning and structure, and especially when we become concerned more with *why* things are and how to live in right relationship with God, the cosmos, the self, and the other, then we realize that truth is not a matter of detachment or objectivity. Objectivity is in itself not a uniquely ideal starting point.

Danish philosopher Søren Kierkegaard speaks of "truth as subjectivity": he doesn't mean that truth is relative, that your truth and my truth can coexist simply because you and I each believe them. Neither does he mean that no objective truth exists, that there is no truth that holds for everyone. He means that objective truth, while important, is not the final aim. Objective truth is just information. The goal is not to find information, or even to discern fact, but to bring ourselves, as living subjects, into engagement with reality, culminating ultimately in a *participation in* the ground of what is real. This engagement—an unabashedly subjective engagement—leads us to what really matters. Of course, it is preferable that the things we engage with passionately are objectively real, rather than personal fantasies or delusions. Subjectivity and objectivity need to remain in some relationship with each other. But the subjectivity of our engagement with reality doesn't make it any less real. Subjectivity, in fact, has played a crucial role in our discernment of reality, and certainly also in our interaction with reality.

It was necessary to say all of this in order to plumb some of the depths of the Christian conviction that the truth is identified with a personal subject, Jesus Christ. Our discernment of and engagement with truth is finally an engagement with the person of Christ. When Pontius Pilate asked Jesus that fateful question, "What is truth?" it is sometimes said that he should better have asked, "*Who* is truth?" because he was standing in the presence of the one who is the truth.

Christianity does not consist in a series of verifiable and interlocking hypotheses. Nor is it a philosophical system consisting in satisfactory, mutually consistent propositions. Our approach has to be different. It's not that we suspend our rational minds—not at all. And Christianity does make sense and has self-consistency. But the way that truth is sought and engaged with is not through detachment but through a living relationship of faith and love with the object we seek. *Credo ut intelligam*: I believe in order to know. I love in order to know. The Scriptures speak of loving the truth (2 Thess 2.10; Zech 8.19), because love and engagement are bound together with knowledge.

Truth, faith, love, and knowledge. They are inextricably linked, because truth is relational; truth is personal.

The Love of "the Law"

The personalization of truth was not exactly a new idea, even during the New Testament era. The Old Testament Wisdom literature (e.g., the book of Proverbs and the Wisdom of Solomon) shows that, especially in the three or four centuries before the coming of Christ, in a hellenized Near East, Wisdom could be personified, as a "she" (e.g., Prov 1.20; 4.6; 7.4; and 9.1) or an "I" (Prov 8.22–31). The authors of these books understood that a relationship with a "she" or a "he" is going to be very different from a relationship with an "it."

Earlier still, when the Hebrews were given the law, their approach to it wasn't exactly personalized, but something of a personal relationship developed between them and the Torah. They did not see the law as a code, much less an arbitrary set of rules to be followed. They saw it as a help, a treasure, and a blessing. They also saw it as an expression of reality—the way things are, the way they are ordered in relation to each other and to their Creator. The Hebrews, who sang "Thy law is truth" (Ps 119.142 LXX), felt it natural that any sane person would consider the law as something he would want to get to know, the way he would want to come to understand life itself and its meaning: "How sweet are thy words to my taste, sweeter than honey to my mouth! Through thy precepts I get understanding" (Ps 119.103).

The law, for the Hebrew, was an object of love. The first of the psalms says that the blessed or happy person delights in the law of the Lord and meditates on it day and night. Such a person is like a tree planted by streams of water that yields its fruit in its season and whose leaf does not wither. In all that he does, he prospers. That is because in understanding the law, he understands what is what, and as a result he is at peace with others, with God, and with himself; he is strong and sure.

Look at Psalm 19.7–10:

> The law of the LORD is perfect, reviving the soul;
> the testimony of the LORD is sure, making wise the
>   simple;
> the precepts of the LORD are right, rejoicing the heart;
> the commandment of the LORD is pure, enlightening the
>   eyes;
> the fear of the LORD is clean, enduring forever;
> the ordinances of the LORD are true, and righteous
>   altogether.
> More to be desired are they than gold, even much fine
>   gold;
> sweeter also than honey, and drippings of the
>   honeycomb.

This certainly sounds different from the average approach today to law or dogma.

Early Christians approached Jesus Christ and the teaching about him (dogma) in the same way that Jews approached the law. Even as St Paul taught that the person of Christ, and life in Christ, supercedes the law, his Epistles began to define who Christ is, how he is both divine and human, and how God exists eternally with his divine Son and his most holy Spirit. Even as the disciples and the first Christians were primarily concerned with praising God (Lk 24.51–53) and spreading the faith, they were also concerned with discerning the truth about God and his Christ, and developing and widening the implications of that truth. It was the birth of Christian dogma.

Christians sing about this dogma as the Jews sang about the law. To this day, for example, when we celebrate St John Chrysostom, one of the Church's great preachers and interpreters, we sing with familiar imagery: "He pours forth sweet streams of dogma like honey for the refreshment of the World." This is why we call him Chrysostom, which means "golden mouth," because his mouth produced beautiful and precious dogma. Similar images for dogma and the law arise again and again through the Church's first millennium.

Dogma (general truth) or dogmas (which are expressions of that truth) do not describe a code, a set of fixed and sterile rules. Rather, dogma describes and defines reality, what is. Dogmas give a true understanding of God, creation, and human personhood. They orient our lives. From dogma, we derive an understanding of reality, an ethos of life, an understanding of how to live, how to stand in relationship with God, the cosmos, the other, and the self. In other words, they tell us how to "do the truth."

To live in harmony with God, with the world, with others, and with ourselves, we need this. We want it. It's our lifeline, our gold, our refreshment, our honey. We ask for it in the liturgy all the time. Again, "Blessed are you, O Lord, teach me your statutes. Blessed are you, O Master, make me to understand your commandments. Blessed are you, O Holy One, enlighten me with your precepts."

Christian dogma truly defines, rightly describes what is. It's the *Church's* dogma, intended in the first instance for those within the

Church (as distinct from *kerygma*, the preaching to those outside). But its truth is universal. If dogma described anything less than the ultimate reality of things, then the whole Church, its teachings and its life, would be nothing more than a sociological phenomenon, perhaps a cult, not worthy of attention other than from cultural anthropologists or psychologists. If Christian dogma didn't teach actual truth, if the Church weren't founded on the bedrock of reality itself, it would be a mere dispenser, alternately, of comfort and guilt.

It is often said that people cling to religion, and Christianity specifically, because it makes life easier, it gives life purpose, meaning. Perhaps most of all, it eases the main anxiety underlying human existence: the fear of death. Anybody for whom the sting of death has been softened is a happier person than the one who lives in constant angst because of his mortality.

It's also sometimes said that religion in general, and Christianity specifically, is good simply because it has been the basis of so much of the world's culture. If we think of how much of history's greatest music, art, and literature were inspired by religious thought, we are indeed awed by the greatness of that contribution. But does this constitute a reason to believe?

Nicholas Arseniev, an Orthodox Renaissance man of the twentieth century, emphasized just this—that the culture, as well as the sense of meaning, purpose, and comfort provided by Christianity, is by itself insufficient reason to be religious. All this is not why we should believe in God, for it's only an accessory, not of decisive importance. We should be ready to give up all the advantages of a religious outlook if it's based on a fundamental untruth or error. The reason it is necessary to believe in God, the only reason which embraces all others, is that this is truth. This is reality, the decisive, fundamental reality, and life-giving truth.[9]

Christianity is not merely an inspirer of good feeling or good art. We would be petty and utilitarian, we would be fools, to believe it for those reasons alone. If it's not true, if it doesn't bring us into communion with the basis of life itself, let's all save ourselves the trouble and respectfully look elsewhere.

It's also said about religion, especially Christianity, that humanity has created God in its own image, that we've in fact created a God who is a kind of wish fulfillment, a God who satisfies our psychological needs. We believe, again because it feels good, because ultimately it makes us happier, even if that happiness is strangely bound up with the guilt and self-flagellation people associate with religion, especially Christianity.

But Christianity teaches that it's the other way around: that *we* are created in *God's* image. Interestingly, the results can be similar: it feels right, in the deepest level of our being, to believe in God and to give thanks to and glorify God. But this is because we are made that way, in a mysterious resemblance to God. Like seeks like, or more accurately in our case, images seek their archetype, beings seek their source and foundation, aliens seek their true home. Furthermore, if it feels good or right to understand the human person as body and soul, to believe in the eternal kingdom of God and to see our lives in these terms, it is because this is the truth about things. Anyone who says that Christians believe because it makes them feel good has at least to entertain the possibility that this good feeling might actually be the result of believing the *truth* and being

[9]Nicholas Arseniev, *Revelation of Life Eternal* (1963; Crestwood, NY: St Vladimir's Seminary Press, 1982), 14.

in relationship with the one who is the ground of our being. Believing the truth might put you in disharmony with a large portion of society, but it puts you into a profound harmony with the cosmos and with its Creator.

Of course, delusions can make people feel good too. And once again, there is no external, universally verifiable evidence that can prove beyond doubt that the position of Christian faith is the position of absolute truth. But the person who seriously calls himself or herself a Christian, one who believes in Jesus Christ as the way, the truth, and the life, is making the statement that this is no delusion: it is *true*.

chapter two
TRUTH AND RELATIVISM: IS ANYBODY WRONG?

P roclaiming that Jesus Christ is *the* truth sounds exclusive. Well, it is, and it isn't. There's a profoundly inclusive dimension to identifying Jesus with the truth, for it affirms and includes everyone and everything that is true, just, beautiful, and good. The other part of that claim, however, is that together with all that is true, there exist things that are untrue, unjust, ugly, and bad. Furthermore, if Jesus is the truth, then salvation—the promise of eternal life in communion with God himself through knowledge of the truth (1 Tim 2.4)—comes through Jesus Christ alone.

How should the Christian be properly inclusive as well as properly exclusive? Postmodern theorists have shown that the definition of any group, system, or theory depends to some extent on the exclusion of another group, system, or theory. That makes sense: defining implies marking out boundaries. But how do Christians mark out their boundaries among other religions and theories?

The previous chapter began to establish both Christian uniqueness and Christian universality. This chapter will focus on Christian uniqueness, dealing with two underlying questions. The first concerns whether you can assert that any religious truth is absolute and universal, or that any religious statement is true while another is false. Here I will seek to establish that it's possible to hold one religious claim as true, knowing that to do so may well mean saying that a conflicting one is false. This proposition, however, follows from the second and larger question of whether we can know anything at all for certain. I will present some of the arguments for and against the idea of absolute reality—and the possibility that it is knowable. Naturally, I can only scratch the surface of centuries of reflection on such matters. But I do hope to emerge from this broad inquiry with a clear and sustainable position.

Aside from being a citizen of my particular time and place—the twenty-first-century West—I am led to many of my questions, as well as some of my answers, by conversations with friends and family, many of whom are either decidedly non-Christian or have fallen away from a committed involvement with the Church. On those occasions when we talk in some serious way about my status as a believing Christian, it's interesting to see what people find most shocking. The words "committed Christian" or "believing Christian" have become so common that nobody really thinks on what they mean. So my partners in conversation can be shocked to realize that I actually believe this stuff to be the truth about God and the world. It's all the more repulsive to people when the implications are teased out: "Does believing this to be the truth mean that you believe that contradictory teachings are *wrong*?"

The conversation often runs along the following lines:

> Friend: The whole area of religion rests on mystery, by definition. After all, as the title of the cult film puts it, "What the *bleep* do we know?" Furthermore, there are

many different religions, and all of them seem to include equally wise people. To me, that means that all religious truth claims are equally valid.

Self: Well, many religious claims may be valid; many may be quite true. But I don't believe them all to be equally true. In fact, I believe some of them are simply false.

F: I find that really outrageous! Don't you realize how offensive that is to other faith traditions? Do you believe that you are wiser than the world's billions of Buddhists, Hindus, and Muslims?

S: This isn't a question of mine or anyone's wisdom. And it's not as if we all disagree on everything—not even nearly. You and I have spoken many times about all of the convergences among the many religious traditions. But there are certain points where we simply can't all be right. And one of these main points centers on Jesus Christ. Is he God's unique Word, the Savior of the world, or is he not?

F: Does it have to be yes or no? Aren't there gradations of agreement on the matter, some of which would be less absolute?

S: Yes, I'd admit gradations. But notice that with each greater affirmation about Jesus, you leave behind certain traditions, certain teachings, and come to a point that is absolute. For example, just about everyone agrees Jesus was a good man. He taught love, he cared especially for the poor and disenfranchised, and he died a voluntary—and perhaps even sacrificial—death. Then you narrow things: He was a prophet. He was a great prophet. He was a "son of God" in that what he spoke was a real message from God. He was *the* Son of God, the Savior of the world, the Messiah foretold by the Hebrew prophets, the way, the truth, and the life, fully sharing in God's own divinity.

By the time you get to these last statements you are a Christian, and decisively not a Muslim, Jew, Buddhist, or Hindu. At that point, if you really believe it, then you *dis-agree* with a statement such as, "Jesus is related to God but in no way beyond how Moses, Buddha, Mohammed, or Mother Teresa were related to God." You believe that such a statement is wrong.

F: So you're saying, for example, that all of Judaism is wrong? Don't you realize that anti-Semitism is based on this attitude?

S: I believe that the view that Jesus is not the promised Messiah is an incorrect view. Is that belief in itself violent to Judaism? There's a difference between being non-Semitic and being anti-Semitic; otherwise simply being a believing Christian would by definition be anti-Semitic. Can I not believe that someone's tradition is mistaken on a key point, without being hateful or violent about it?

F: No, I don't believe you can, because your belief—or rather your conviction—is an ideological violence to the other. That kind of violence leads in an unbroken contin-uum to hatred and physical violence. You know, Peter, I really can't believe that a thinking person today can be as intolerant as this. Haven't human beings lived through enough in history to realize that anything we say or believe has to be provisional, that it's always possible that we are wrong? Furthermore, haven't you read enough critical theory to be convinced that there can only be truths within and for particular communities? The claim to universality is simply childish.

S: Of *course* I can be wrong, and maybe I am. But I don't think so, and I would be lying if I said I did.

Here the dialogue may continue along more or less interesting lines of reasoning.

At the heart of the argument is the difference between absolutism and relativism. We'll need to define those words very carefully. *Absolutism*, in one dictionary definition, is synonymous with despotism and tyranny, or the political theory that all authority ought to be exercised by one person. But it can also mean "belief in absolute principles in politics, philosophy, or theology."[1] One definition is pejorative, the other neutral. One of my goals is to show that they are not necessarily entwined, that belief in absolute truth does not lead inexorably to despotism and tyranny, and neither does it lead to the erasure of nuance.

Some people prefer to avoid the word absolutism altogether, even when they believe in the existence of absolute truth and absolute principles. Avoiding it is not a bad idea. Generally, we ought to be cautious of "isms": they signal ideologies. But then what about

---

[1] "Absolutism," in Judy Pearsall, ed., *The Concise Oxford Dictionary* (Oxford: Oxford Univ. Press, 1999).

relativism? Well, one of my chief points in this chapter is that relativism, which claims to be nothing but neutrality and tolerance, is an ideology that can be as tyrannical as any other.

So for the purposes of this book, let absolutism be "the belief in the existence and knowability of absolute truth and of absolute principles of right and wrong." Truths, and likewise moral principles, do exist which apply to everyone and everything, and they can be known. Not every principle is absolute, but some are.

Relativism, more or less the opposite of absolutism, is the view that all knowledge is relative. For the purposes of this book, I define relativism as the belief that either there is no absolute truth (and even no external world at all, only our perceptions and mental concepts) or there is no certain knowledge of absolute truth. It therefore entails the belief that truth and moral principles are relative: what's true or right for me is not necessarily true or right for you.

Note that relativism should not be confused with the subjective nature of truth and its pursuit discussed earlier. To say that the understanding of truth is by nature subjective—because it involves a genuine personal engagement with things—is different from saying that truth is by nature relative. Relativism holds that my engagement with things dictates only my own personal truth, and that absolute truth itself cannot be apprehended or is nonexistent.

Relativism as Worldview

Both absolutism and relativism are beliefs. Ironically, those who hold the relativist view are the most reluctant to call their position a position at all, much less acknowledge that it's a belief.

They believe it to be the truth about things. This explains why sometimes, ironically, relativists can sound absolutist about their relativism.

My friend in the above conversation is thoroughly convinced that her position is not a mere proposition or belief but inescapable reality; namely, that to insist on one truth over another is intellectually and morally impoverished. Relativists believe that theirs is a view beyond views, a theory beyond theories. But relativist worldviews are just that: worldviews. Forms of relativism have figured prominently in the academic and political culture of the West in recent decades and have largely been established as the way to view our existence. Yet relativist views are part of the history of ideas. This lineage doesn't prove or disprove relativism; it just shows that it's one point of view among others.

Relativism involves a combination of related skepticisms: one is doubt about the existence of a single absolute truth or reality; the other is doubt about the possibility of knowing reality, or whether it even exists. The conclusion in either case is that convictions—about things seen or unseen—are provisional. The maximum you can logically assert is that you believe something, but that another person's belief, however much it contradicts your own, has an equal chance of being true. The maximum you can achieve for an ethical code is a moral pragmatism—a code of individual and corporate behavior that, according to experience, serves most people well.

Skepticism about absolute reality goes back some 2500 years, to the pre-Socratic Greek philosophers. In the fifth century B.C., Zeno and his teacher Parmenides had already taught that our perceptions of the world are just illusions. Protagoras in his turn said, "Man is the measure of all things—of things that are, that they are, of things that are not, that they are not." Plato's memorable analogy of the cave suggests that what we perceive and experience here is like a dim shadow of reality, that this world is a poor copy of a perfected realm of ideas. His views formed the underpinnings of the intellectual life of Western civilization for centuries.

Millennia later, in the seventeenth and eighteenth centuries, philosophers began taking a renewed interest in these early Greek thinkers and produced systematic philosophies based on certain principles: that all we know are our own perceptions and that there's no guarantee that our perceptions correspond to any objective reality. At this point, Rene Descartes concluded that there is only one absolute truth that underlies all truth: his own existence. Descartes thinks, and therefore he is; on this he founded his entire principle of knowledge. He put everything into doubt, except the conviction of the one truth: the fact that he is thinking.

The question that occupied the major thinkers of Descartes' era was, How do you bridge the gap between reality and our perceptions of reality? Idealists believed that there is no external reality, only our perceptions. Realists held that there is a reality, and our perceptions may correspond to it. Empiricists, some of whom believed in God, continued to ground their philosophy in human perception and in their faith in the laws of nature. They had come full circle with the pre-Socratics: "Man is the measure of all things." They developed a moral philosophy that was also human-centered, based effectively on what makes the most people happy.

By the twentieth century, the lingering question as to whether there is an absolute reality, and whether we can really know it, became increasingly bound up with reflection on language: What is the relationship between words and the things they are supposed to represent? How can we be sure that our words convey to others anything resembling the meaning that we give them? (More on this later.) The serious inquiry into whether language can reliably convey meaning represents something of a climax in this line of reasoning, which suspects that there may in fact be no correspondence between reality and our thoughts and words.

Add to this the increased influence on the West of Eastern religions, many of which carry a built-in openness to other views. Although Hinduism and Buddhism, in their various forms, do make exclusive claims and have clear moral principles, Buddhist doctrine, for example, precludes the notion of God or even of the self as a reality which actually exists. That leaves some things pretty open-ended.

This trajectory of skepticism (which I've summarized in an extremely simplistic way) joins an ever-increasing awareness of different cultures and their religious and moral codes. The more we learn about the world, and the more that people become interconnected across cultures through media and communication, the more we see that different people view reality through their particular frameworks. It doesn't take a professional philosopher to see this. People who travel, people who open their eyes to others living around them in an increasingly pluralistic society, and even people who frequent Internet blogs, can see that there are many, varying understandings of reality, both physical and spiritual, and many ways of structuring an ethical or moral code. Given this evidence, relativism concludes that no view of reality, no moral code, can be privileged over any other.

Religious Relativism

Having developed in this way as an idea within the history of ideas, relativism arrived in Western religious belief. Religious relativism holds that, by definition, nobody can claim to have the right perspective to the exclusion of another perspective. One example: Anglican philosopher and theologian John Hick has suggested the analogy of the planets (representing world religions) orbiting the sun (representing truth). Each planet receives the warmth and light from the one sun in their own way. No one of the planets can lay an exclusive claim to the light, or even any particularly special possession of it. The light is inexhaustible and therefore not fully apprehensible, and it distributes itself indiscriminately.

I should be clear at the outset of this portion of my reflection that I will use John Hick at several points below, primarily because he is a prominent and articulate spokesman who provides many evocative metaphors for a relativist-pluralist position. My use of him, however, will not do justice to the wide and variegated body of literature which tries to make sense of the existence of multiple religious faiths. It won't even do justice to the breadth and complexity of his own thought. I will mention some of his more memorable images and examples only in order to indicate where religious relativism is capable of going, for I believe that it is a problematic destination.

Hick's image of the sun in the middle of orbiting planets is a canny extension of Copernicus' revolutionary discovery that the sun, not the earth, stands at the center of our planetary system. In the sixteenth century, people groaned to be parted from their assumption that the earth was the geometrical center of creation and to accept that ours is but one of several planets orbiting the sun. Hick argues that Christians must undergo their own Copernican revolution, surrendering their claims to centrality and universality.

This view does presuppose the existence of an absolute truth, even an absolute God. But it also emphasizes the unknowability of God or truth, and therefore the impossibility of certitude in the exclusive truth of one's beliefs. One can be reasonably sure of one's belief—that's what faith is, after all—but it's not possible to state that one's belief is true to the exclusion of another's. How does this system work itself out? My belief that Jesus Christ is uniquely related to God, being himself divine (as God's Son), may, logically, be correct and true. But it is impossible to *know* that it is right, and therefore it's unreasonable to hold that Jesus Christ is *the* way, *the* truth, and *the* life for everyone. It's also unreasonable to say that the assertions of other faiths, including those incompatible with my claims about Jesus, are wrong.

Religious relativism can also take the form of a looser interpretation of events and teachings. For example, you might say that the incarnation of the Son of God in Jesus of Nazareth is a manifestation of the very same reality expressed in the Hindu concept of the avatar of Vishnu, an avatar being the descent or manifestation of a god. Or you might say that Mohammed's ascent from the Dome of the Rock is spiritually the same event as the ascension of Christ after his resurrection appearances.

What is a person of faith to make of relativism when it is expressed in such terms?

Engaging Religious Relativism

Inclusion, embrace, openness, welcome. The heart may rejoice at a contemplation of these words and what they mean. People of all faiths can rightly celebrate the convergences in their understandings. Despite differences in religious faiths, there's much we hold in common about the human person in relation to God and creation, and about how people ought to live to become enlightened beings. But there are points at which we must admit that we believe different things—and it is not just a matter of how we construe our words. The differences can cut to the core of faith and be truly oppositional.

For example, the Christian asserts that Jesus Christ is the only-begotten Son of God. Spelling this out a bit, we say that God the Father eternally begets a Son (also called his Word) and eternally breathes (or proceeds) a Spirit. The Son and the Spirit are divine, just as God is, and therefore can also be called God. The Son and the Spirit are persons other than God the Father himself but nonetheless complete his very being, so that he is One God—not despite but because of their existence.

The Muslim asserts, "Allah is He on Whom all depend. He begets not, nor is He begotten. And none is like Him" (Quran 112.1–4). Islam is founded on, among other things, the unipersonal nature of God; it explicitly excludes the teaching that God begets or that one who is called God could be begotten.

While it's always beneficial to explore another's terminology and there may be greater agreement than at first seems apparent, there appears to be a bona fide disagreement between these two positions. They say, and mean, different things. In the first, God exists in communion with his Son and his Spirit, who are simultaneously other than himself and one with himself. In the second, God is in communion with no other; he is a monad, his oneness is radical, numerical. Logically, both of these positions can't be true.

A pluralist-relativist might say that one of the two positions may indeed be true in an absolute sense. But the pluralist would assert, with certainty, that we cannot say for sure. Given that people of wisdom and piety have drawn their different conclusions based on the same data of life on earth and of whatever divine revelation there is, and given that their conclusions, on the face of it, are equally probable, none of us is in a position to say which one is right.

This form of relativism at least admits that the differences exist. To gloss over these differences, to assert that they are not substantial, is unacceptable. It is illogical, for reasons we'll go into below. But it's also disrespectful to the integrity of both traditions, and it smacks of prideful angelism, observing the millenniums-old traditions of faith from a benevolent distance: "If only they knew—as I know—that the truth lies above and beyond all their beliefs!"

Here is another example of the problems inherent in religious relativism (again from the writing of John Hick). Hick takes note of the following verse from the ancient Rig Veda:

> They call it Indra, Mitra, Varuna, and Agni
> And also heavenly, beautiful Garutman:
> The real is one, though sages name it variously.[2]

[2] 1.164, cited in John Hick, *God and the Universe of Faiths* (London: Macmillan, 1988), 140. The translation runs differently in *The Rig Veda: An Anthology*, trans. W. D. O'Flaherty (New York: Penguin, 1981), 80.

Hick suggests that this Hindu verse might be creatively retranslated into the terms of the faiths in the contemporary pluralistic West:

> They call it Yahweh, Allah, Krishna, Param Atma
> And also holy, blessed Trinity:
> The real is one, though sages name it differently.[3]

This metamorphosis presents profound difficulties. In the first place, a certain violence is done to the Hindu verse. Indra, Mitra, Varuna, and Agni are different gods within the Hindu pantheon, each with different personalities, standing in different relationships to the cosmos. The verse from the Rig Veda testifies to a principle of unity that underlies the differentiation of Hindu gods. It is a classic "enlightenment moment," the kind one finds in all of the great religious traditions, which hinges on the realization of the ultimate unity of being. But in its Hindu usage, the verse is referring to gods from within a single community of faith. To apply this same verse to Yahweh, Allah, Krishna, and the Holy Trinity stretches the intention beyond the breaking point. Hick's pantheon becomes a jumble of deities, some with degrees of overlapping identity, and others, which may refer to entirely different concepts, stemming from different faith communities.

Hick's point is perhaps simpler than I am allowing; he only wants to say that what we name separately is in fact one reality. In that case the Orthodox Christian will have a double problem with his proposition. First, he's making flawed use of the Rig Veda to prove a statement which cannot be true; it's a literary violation in the

---

[3]*God and the Universe of Faiths*, 140.

service of a philosophical one. Second he is making a statement that none of the religious faiths represented could subscribe to.

Arrogance is supposed to be the unique ailment of absolutists in their claims to be right. But are religious pluralists less arrogant in some of their positions? In effect they assert that the ancient religious traditions, all of which hold, to various degrees, that their faith positions are unique, have got it wrong. It's only we enlightened postmodern Westerners who have got it right. We know that there's a truth beyond all their truths, a sun at the center of all their little planets. And we'll use their ancient texts to show how some of them, looking as if through an opaque window, even anticipated this great enlightenment of relativism for which the world was waiting. Christian language can sound just about that arrogant too, and when it does, we have a huge problem. But at least we admit to having a clear-cut worldview, rather than pretending we don't.

Let's look now at some of the potential logical problems of both relativism and Christian absolutism.

Divine Unknowability and the Limits of Language

Going deeper into the logic of religious relativism, we find several more arguments that are used to support the idea that no religious view is correct to the exclusion of another. These fall into two categories: the inherent unknowability of God, and the inherent limitations of human reason and speech. We can't know God and, furthermore, our words fall short of expressing . . . well, *anything*.

Virtually every religion that believes in a supreme deity will assert that its deity is unknowable. The Orthodox Christian says it at every Divine Liturgy: "You are God, ineffable [not describable in words], inconceivable, invisible, and incomprehensible." God is wholly other, beyond knowability. In the language of Pseudo-Dionysius the Areopagite, God is beyond both knowability and unknowability, beyond being, even beyond divinity (*hypertheos*).[4]

God is unknowable by definition. But God is also unknowable to us because of our limitations as created beings. We sing, at the Feast of the Transfiguration, that Christ's glory was revealed to his disciples as "far as they could bear it" or as "far as they were able to see it." Our perception is limited, and certainly our ability to express in words transcendent divinity is limited.

This can easily be taken a step further: our ability to perceive *anything* is limited, as is our ability to express it fully. At any rate, it's impossible to be sure that someone else understands the same thing as we do by our words. Is "red" for you the same thing as "red" for me?

These basic observations are taken still further by the religious relativist, who might be influenced by the assumptions of the logical positivist. Positivism holds that the only things knowable are our own perceptions, which may or may not correspond to reality. It also holds that the only statement that has meaning is one that can be logically proved or disproved.[5] Enter, too, the profound

---

[4]See the introductory prayer in Dionysius' *Mystical Theology*, in Colm Luibheid, trans., *Pseudo-Dionysius: The Complete Works* (New York: Paulist, 1987), 135.

[5]Religious relativists, such as John Hick, again, are often explicit about their positivism: "Any theory that can be of interest to human beings must be capable, in principle at least, of confirmation or disconfirmation within human experience. Otherwise it is 'meaningless' or pointless" (Hick, *God and the Universe of Faiths*, 166).

influence of late twentieth-century literary theory. Even the basic study of text and language shows that identical concepts can be conveyed through different signs, words, and images. Contemporary literary theory is founded on the presupposition that the meaning of any sign or word is relative and that, therefore, there is no certainty that anyone means the same thing as anyone else.

The collective force of God's unknowability and the limitations of language doesn't forbid some relativists from having religious belief, or even from calling themselves Christians. But it does forbid them from being absolutely certain about that belief, and it certainly prohibits them from saying that another belief is false.

In chapter 4 we will look more extensively into how it's possible to speak about the unknowable God. For now, I will just say that an admission of divine mystery and linguistic poverty should not lead us into the paralysis of extreme religious relativism. We should strive instead for an awed humility before God and the certainty that God both reveals himself to us "as far as we can bear it" and endows us with the faculties to receive and process that revelation. It's our responsibility to articulate what we believe God reveals to us about himself and his world and to do so as clearly and honestly as possible while being respectful of the persons who hold alternate views. We are looking for humble certitude—and that's not an oxymoron.

The Excluded Middle

I've given religious relativism a rather hard time, but I don't believe that absolutism can be let off the hook too easily either; some tendencies need to be checked. To begin with, then, let's examine and test an argument invoked by some Christians who believe in absolutes: the law of noncontradiction. This idea, that if one statement is true, then a series of other statements is false, has its roots in Aristotle, who spoke of the "excluded middle." Something cannot be "P" and "not-P" at the same time. The way Aristotle puts it in his *Metaphysics*, "One cannot say of something that it is and that it is not, in the same respect and at the same time."

There are some limitations or qualifiers to the law of noncontradiction, or the excluded middle, some apparent and some real; these have to do with things that somehow *are* both P and not-P at the same time. For example, some people use the phenomenon of light as an example, since light can appear to consist in particles, as well as in waves. Electrons, too, could be seen to behave both as particles and waves. Over time, however, a unified particle-wave theory arose which showed that light only seems to be two incompatibly different things at once; in fact it is simply observed to behave differently under different conditions.

A more important and more genuine exception to the excluded middle rests in the person of Jesus Christ. The law of noncontradiction tells us that he cannot be both God and man at the same time, because man is radically different from God. Indeed, the idea of the incarnation, where God becomes human while not ceasing to be God, therefore being two incompatibly different things at the same time, has contradicted the logical instincts of people since the outset of Christianity. The apparent impossibility for Christ to be described by two contradictory natures, divine and human—or the "folly" of the conclusion that his divinity is shown precisely in his humanity—produced centuries of theological struggles, often intertwined with ecclesiastical and political battles, even unto bloodshed. These struggles were devoted to finding ways of spelling out, in language acceptable at once to the intellect and to the heart, the paradox of the God-man, Jesus Christ. The one who feels hunger, thirst, temptation, sweat, and fear, the one who weeps for his friend Lazarus, is the very same one who was in the beginning with God (Jn 1.1–2), who therefore can say, "Before Abraham was, I AM" (Jn 8.58).

Christianity's answer to the problem of Christ's two natures is complex and multifaceted. One component of the argument is that, while divine and human natures are indeed radically other (the one is uncreated, the other is created), they are also integrally related. That relationship is expressed in the biblical teaching that the human person is made in the image and likeness of God. So when the divine Son of God becomes also human, there's a similitude in nature, a familiarity.

Still, the dual nature of Christ remains a dazzling mystery, for here is one person who is, in Aristotle's language, both P and not-P simultaneously. It's not the only apparent breach of the law of noncontradiction that Christians are expected to embrace. Since Christ partakes of both divine and human natures, Orthodox Christians believe that we human beings also are called to partake of two natures, human and divine. The Church Fathers often repeat that God became everything that we are so that we might become everything that he is.

Our sacramental theology also requires us to accept that single substances participate in dual realities. In our Eucharist the bread and wine become the body and blood of Christ even as they continue to be bread and wine. The elements participate in two realities.

In effect, the Christian is being called to expand his or her understanding of being, or ontology. That understanding applies within some very specific parameters. It has to do entirely with the two-natured person of Christ. The possibility of our becoming divinized humans, of bread becoming body, all of this rests on the P-and-not-P of Jesus Christ. A Christian's ability to see Christ as both divine and human, to see sacramental elements as both bread and Christ, does not entail that Christians should dismiss all P-and-not-P situations as noncontradictory. God cannot be both trinitarian and unipersonal, as Christians and Muslims respectively would have it. He cannot be both a personal, relational being and simultaneously impersonal and nonrelational, as Christians and Buddhists respectively would have it. These are different registers that cannot be forced into relation.

Apparent Opposites and Genuine Contradiction

In the doctrine of the incarnation and in many other spheres of life, we can see the potential for the truth of two apparently contradictory statements. Even in the words of our Lord we find mixed messages. On the one hand he says, "He who is not against us is for us" (Mk 9.40), but we also hear him say, "He who is not with me is against me" (Mt 12.30). He tells us that "the gate is narrow and the way is hard that leads to life, and those who find it are few" (Mt 7.14), but then he says, "My yoke is easy [or good], and my burden is light" (Mt 11.30), and "In my Father's house are many rooms" (Jn 14.2). With each of these statements we can say, "Yes, I can see how this is true." And yet they seem to contradict each other.

This leads us to a few more observations. One is that sometimes apparent contradictions are simply things that hold true on different levels, or in different contexts, and identifying such cases where they exist doesn't make one into a full-blown relativist. There is a sense in which the gate is narrow indeed, and the kingdom must be taken by force. The way of the cross is the way of voluntary suffering unto death. But there's also a sense in which there are many rooms, that the way is easy, and that the cross represents Christ's open arms, receiving with the widest embrace there is. These "opposites" are all true if we are willing to take each point in its context and balance it with the other side. There's a time for the inclusiveness of "he who is not against us is for us," and a time for the clear excision of "he who is not with me is against me." Didn't someone once say there's a time to weep, and a time to laugh; a time to keep silence, and a time to speak; a time to break down, and a time to build up (Eccl 3.1–8)?

A related point: just because absolute principles exist doesn't mean that every principle is absolute. Many facets of our complex lives seem contradictory but when viewed from a different perspective are shown to agree. The entire Christian message is in this sense contradictory: "Lo, through the cross, joy has come into the world," meaning that through this instrument of torture, the world is filled with light and gladness. It is the way of divine Providence that good may come through ill. Simone Weil, who was religiously thorough in exploring contradictions, gives the image of walking a mountain path and seeing a forest, and then a lake, and then ascending higher to be able to see both.[6]

Vital as it is to reject religious relativism, it is equally important to underscore the proper boundaries of absolutism. Radicalism

[6]Simone Weil, *Gravity and Grace*, trans. Gustave Thibon (Lincoln, NE: Univ. of Nebraska Press, 1997), 152.

and religious fundamentalism both grow out of the practice of lifting every statement to the level of the absolute. Orthodox Christians—especially those who are fleeing the relativism of society or their former religious affiliations, seeking refuge in the unequivocal absoluteness of Orthodoxy—are not immune from this danger. We meet Orthodox Christians who argue with nearly the same fervor about the Julian or the Revised Julian Calendar as about the divinity and humanity of Christ. Orthodox Christianity is a strange and yet realistic blend of absolute firmness in its dogmatic teachings and practices and absolute catholicity and balance. Ever mindful of the complexity of human life, seminary professor Serge Verhovskoy would repeatedly tell his students, "Orthodoxy is the absence of one-sidedness." The "gestalt" of Orthodoxy, which simultaneously rejects relativism and sectarian one-sidedness, is not easy to apprehend; we must spend our lives in it in order to begin to find our way. Our exploration of the formation of doctrine in the second part of this book may go a certain distance on the way to such a beginning.

Language and Shared Meanings

The law of noncontradiction may be clear enough in itself, but it depends on the assurance that two people discussing an issue are talking on the same plane, about the same thing. It implies a common definition of terms. The following two sentences would appear to be at odds:

* The human person has a soul.

* The human person has no soul.

If they are at odds, or if they are in fact not, has everything to do with how one defines soul, not to mention how one conceives of "having" a soul.

Any meaningful discourse has to be founded on a shared definition of terms. In fact, the law of noncontradiction, stating that something cannot be P and not-P at the same time, rests on an agreed-on definition of P. There are important implications, then, to being able to demonstrate that two people can come to a shared understanding of any word or idea. A signifier (a word, sign, or name) needs to be shown to be signifying the same thing, the same reality, for those two people.

Postmodern literary theory is right to distinguish the signifier from the thing signified, and thus to remind people that they may be talking about different things with the same words. But when postmodern theory concludes that persons can *never* be confident that they mean the same thing by the same words, then it becomes wrong-headed and nihilistic. A more viable conclusion understands the role of communion between persons. For persons are not atoms but beings in communion. Agreed-on definitions increase in likelihood within specific communities. The meaning of words is constituted by the way they are used. In order to make sense of a word like *soul* in the statement "The human person has a soul," one needs to see how the word operates within the community and framework in which it is spoken. If an Orthodox Christian is saying that human beings have souls, then you need to look at the ways the word soul is used within Orthodox Christian thought.

It's useful if two people make sure that they are talking about the same thing before they conclude that they agree or disagree with each other. Take, for example, the controversy around the fifth-century council of Chalcedon, which resulted in a major church division that plagues us to this day. The revisiting of this disagreement during the late twentieth century is tending to show that the two church families, divided for a millennium and a half, hadn't essentially disagreed: they just meant different things by the same words, and the same things by different words.[7] Attentiveness to the shared meaning of words is vitally important, and all the more so across communities of faith, culture, and language. But given that attention, genuine communication is, in fact, possible. And this means that genuine agreement and genuine disagreement are also possible.

Truth in and for the Community

Shared definitions within a community are one thing. We come to another question when we consider shared *values* within and between communities. For just as the use of language will vary from community to community, so will beliefs and moral principles. That observation leads some to conclude that no community may question or cast judgment on the beliefs or moral principles of any other.

There is a kind of basic wisdom to this, as in "When in Rome, do as the Romans do," or (the Russian Orthodox analog), "Don't go to someone else's monastery with your own set of rules." But this principle must not be taken to an extreme. U.S. law may allow certain Native American tribes to use illegal drugs in their ancient religious ceremonies, but if those tribes were to sell such drugs on the street, the law would react.

[7] I am of course presenting a simplified account of a complex historic controversy and a complex process of rapprochement.

These questions are especially relevant in the area of human rights. A degree of relativism—in the sense of cultural sensitivity—can be a positive thing. It can serve as a much-needed corrective to cultural imperialism, which for centuries has been so destructive around the world. But it becomes counterproductive when sensitivity becomes a god, eclipsing fundamental and, yes, absolute human rights to life and dignity. People of different cultures have a responsibility to be deeply critical of the once-common practice of female infanticide in China; they may justly decry the practice of dowry burnings in India; they should be outraged at "honor killings" in sectors of the Islamic world. These examples may be too obvious, but there are those who would relativize even such practices. We need to be alert to the more subtle erosions of moral truth that clear the way for genuinely egregious ones. "It's their culture, therefore it's valid for them" can be applied, but we must discern its limits: relativism can also be paralyzing, or more dramatically put, it has the potential for a homicidal sensitivity. The biggest problem with a thoroughgoing relativism may not even be the logical one. It's that relativism shrinks from admitting the existence of real evil.

Absolute Truth and Violence

It's time to close this chapter. I'd like to leave it on a critically important note: the distinction between tolerance and relativism and between violence and absolutism.

We are familiar with, and have directly or indirectly reviewed, several arguments that are commonly invoked against absolute truth and absolute moral principles. One is that people who hold to these absolutes must be intellectually impoverished. A related one is that belief in absolutes is archaic; it has failed to undergo the Copernican revolution. An argument we need to address further is that belief in absolutes, and firm religious conviction in general, necessarily leads to violence or simply *is* violence.

The problem is that firmly believing Christians, as well as strong adherents to other faiths, do have some explaining to do. The fact that people kill each other because of religious disagreement is surely one of the greatest of all tragedies. Christians need to do more than offer explanations; we need to offer personal and communal repentance. Repentance here means acknowledging that violence against others because they believe differently or belong to a different community is a terrible sin.

Religious belief, and belief in the truth of one's claims, needs to be part and parcel of an enlivening of the soul, an opening of the heart, a commitment to reason and dialogue. Sadly, it often runs in tandem with the opposite tendencies, a hardening of the heart, violence. This is dreadful beyond words. But we shouldn't swear off religion because of it. To *identify* religious belief, and specifically belief in absolute truth, with violence and the hardening of the heart is not only illogical; it is horribly misleading.

In each case of historical or present-day religious violence, we must make a crucial distinction between the belief and the violence. To use the tired but useful metaphor, we must distinguish between the baby and the bathwater.

I've heard from several fine and thoughtful people that "given the Holocaust, we have to reevaluate our truth claims about Jesus Christ." No. Given the Holocaust, we have to reevaluate human evil. We have to look at how people abuse the cult of personality, at the mob mentality, at the concept of racial purity. We have to confront evil in societies. And very definitely we have to look at the evil in our own selves, because none of us is immune to hatred. Given religious violence, we also have to reevaluate religious language, the way we speak to each other, and even the way we speak about Jesus Christ.

But if we adjust our truth claims, we do throw out the baby with the bathwater. People certainly abuse religious belief, but what needs to change is not the belief but the abuse. Taking as the truth the Gospels' portrayal of Jesus and his unique role in human salvation does not inexorably lead to abuse or evil. Human sin, in the form of lust for power, pride, and blindness to the other, may seize upon Jesus' words as a vehicle for violence. When it does, kill the sin, not Jesus.

Some will argue that they are not equating religious conviction with religious violence. Instead they are simply showing that absolutism in and of itself is already an ideological violence and leads systemically to a more tangible violence. This assertion is harder to contest, since the world's despots and terrorists have generally preached absolute principles, often religious ones. But we might observe that it's harder to locate the innumerable healthy exponents of firm and clear religious belief, because it's the unhealthy ones who call attention to themselves. We mustn't let the fanatics define what genuine religious conviction is all about.

Is there a way to renounce relativism while renouncing violence? A way of promoting genuine tolerance, sensitivity, and love without reevaluating our truth claims? I am fervently convinced that there is. We must work constantly to find that way and articulate it, because religious people do have a lot to repent of, seeing the violence we really have done to other people, whether with weapons or with words.

The Church puts before us the way of the martyr: rather than kill for the truth, let yourself be killed for the truth. It needn't go to the point of physical killing, but it certainly can. We must die to religious pride, even as we would die for our genuine and godly religious zeal. Again, humble zeal, like humble certitude, isn't an oxymoron. There is such a thing as enlightened zeal, as well as unenlightened zeal (Rom 10.2).

The Church's history also shows us the way of dialogue, where again we must steer a careful course. We have to be genuine listeners, presume the other's good intentions, be willing to see truth in the other's position, be willing to enrich and deepen our own faith, and be alert to the possibility that our supposed disagreements may in reality be a question of the definition of words or a difference in perception. We even have to be open to seeing where we have gotten it wrong, where our expressions or our behavior have failed to be true to the genuine apostolic Christian teaching. At the same time, we must be true to our convictions in the essentials of our faith, willing to identify points of genuine disagreement and to consider their implications. It is a subtle course indeed, but it is a true one. And it is possible, by God's grace.

As much as we need to be mindful that our own absolute belief doesn't spill over into violence, what happens when we encounter others whose absolute belief is expressed in violence or oppression? Christian and other religious minorities in parts of the world are subject to gross intolerance and human rights violations in the name of religious conviction. This is all the more a time to tell the world that religious conviction need not, and emphatically must not, be expressed violently, even as the conviction itself remains uncompromised.

Conclusions

Both absolutism and relativism have their uses and their dangers. Just as absolutism need not lead to violence under the guise of religious belief, relativism likewise does not necessarily lead to spinelessness or condescension under the guise of compassion and enlightenment. The key is to be alert to the pitfalls and potential of each starting point. Nonetheless, this chapter has attempted to address primarily some of the problems of relativism in general, and religious relativism in particular:

✳ It's important to unmask relativism's pretense of standing above and beyond all beliefs, convictions, and ideologies. Relativism's disguise as tolerant enlightenment instead of an ideology alongside others has helped to embed it deeply into society and the universities. Relativism itself is a worldview with specific presuppositions.

✳ Some of these presuppositions are logically incoherent and lead to unsustainable positions, such as an unwillingness to admit that some truth claims and some moral principles are simply incompatible.

✳ Absolutism does not have a monopoly on arrogance. Relativism's claim to embrace all of the world's great faiths are potentially at least as arrogant and sometimes just as absolutist.

✳ Those of us who hold to absolute principles and beliefs need to see where some apparently incompatible claims in fact *can* both be true, in different senses and different contexts. We have to be alert to our potential for absolutizing things that should not be absolutized.

In all, we must be able to believe that individual people, and entire groups of people, hold views that are wrong. What's perhaps harder for some of us is that we must also be prepared to be shown where *we* are wrong. Both of these things, however, are possible only if we believe that there is an absolute right and wrong, an absolute truth, and that human beings have the capacity to come to know that truth. In our society today, it is becoming an act of courage to say as much.

chapter three
TRUTH AND STORY:
DOES HISTORY MATTER?

S
ome years ago I was in the midst of a long and relaxed conversation with a good friend—a priest and scholar from Russia. Then, as the conversation took an uncomfortable turn, tension filled the room. We were talking about some of the Old Testament accounts—I think they were about Noah and Job—and I remarked that I couldn't understand why some people absolutely insist that these events occurred exactly as written. "Why do some people need to believe that every one of these stories actually happened, as if they could be captured on a video camera?"

But it turned out that this was in fact his position. "How could you suggest that they didn't happen?" he said. "They are in the *Bible!*" To him it was blasphemy to suggest that these are "mere stories." "Are you saying that everyone who has believed in these accounts throughout history has been wrong? That you are smarter than they are?" He was shocked and bothered, and so was I, by how our discussion was turning out. "Next thing you'll tell me," he said, "is that Jesus wasn't historical? That he didn't live or die or rise from the dead?"

I said, "No, I won't tell you any such thing. Because I believe as you do, that Jesus did live, die, and rise from the dead. Jesus' life, death, and resurrection are exactly what all the scriptural narratives point to. Let me ask you, though, why the "historic fact" of these stories is so important to you. It seems to me that the Fathers were primarily interested in the stories themselves, rather than their historicity."

He then took a more positive tack. "Do you know how I know that these things actually happened, that Adam and Job and Jonah and Noah really lived through exactly what is written about them? It is because I am a priest, and I hear confessions. And I hear these very stories lived out in the lives of people who tell me their lives. I hear Job in the poor woman who lost her husband and son in Chechnya. I hear Jonah in the seminarian who is considering abandoning his studies . . ."

I was stunned to hear him say this. "Father! You've just cited one of the main reasons why the question of whether they actually happened *doesn't* matter. They are true stories." And so our conversation steered onto a new track.

This dialogue introduces an inquiry about the different ways truth may be conveyed. It opens an exploration of history, story, parable, and myth. But it also suggests that one of the chief reasons to be interested in such an inquiry is that—for better or for worse—it's at the heart of how we "moderns" read Scripture as well as other texts, such as the lives of the saints. In the second portion of this book we will devote attention to Scripture and Tradition and the whole "hermeneutic question" (the matter of how we interpret these things). But for now, we are well poised to explore story and history.

One reason that this is a timely question is that the reading of Scripture, especially some of its key passages, is highly contested between people who accord it supreme authority and those who don't, as well as among Christians of the same denomination. Look at how differently people read the creation narratives in the book of Genesis.[1] In contemporary American society, the question of how literally we read the first three chapters of Genesis is fiercely debated among people of all backgrounds. Some insist that Genesis is God's word *and therefore* represents an accurate historical and geological-astrological account of the world's coming into being. Others, who may or may not feel bound by the Judeo-Christian tradition and its scriptural texts, consider themselves bound to a doctrine of evolution which is "sheerly scientific" *and therefore* true. The logic in each of these cases needs to be called into question but rarely is. In the media and in the public square, the debate almost never allows for a more nuanced position that is both deeply religious (and traditional) and open to a variety of views on the astrophysical and biological origins of the cosmos.

Now, this chapter does not aim to settle the question of the genesis of the universe or of the human person, to make a ruling in favor of evolution or creation or "intelligent design." But the creation narratives will come up several times as a backdrop against which to consider a series of questions concerning the truth and how it is conveyed.

Here are the questions that will occupy us:

---

[1] I use "narratives" in the plural, distinguishing the six-day account from the Paradise account that begins at Genesis 2:4b.

* Can truth be conveyed through stories? Can stories be true if they are not based on events?

* What is history, and how do different kinds of literature tell it?

* How did the scriptural and other ancient authors consider such questions?

* How does a reader today interact with texts that came from a very different sensibility on such questions?

Modern Sensibilities

Let's examine the particular way in which people today tend to engage such questions, because a chapter such as this would have taken different form in an age before our own, and although it could be argued that it would change again not too far into the future, it is necessary today.

Our curiosity about the historicity of the biblical narratives constitutes a relatively new line of inquiry. Specifically, the "historicity question" took on a new character after the eighteenth-century Enlightenment. There are many factors involved in the rise of this concern over the past couple of centuries, among them an exponential increase in literacy and, more recently, the rise of information sharing and technology and the widespread availability of multiple accounts of events. We have come to look at the past, and especially accounts of and stories about the past, from a critical perspective. We have come to apply a scientific approach (one based on history and fact) to literature of all kinds, and that approach can do violence to Scripture's genuine spirit and meaning.[2] We see this especially in the scientific or historical-critical approach, which holds the promise of informing us about what Scripture "really says," or about "Scripture as fact," yet misses the point of Scripture.

The problem of "scientific historiography" is that it draws much clearer lines between history and story, myth and fact, than the ancient authors did. People attempt to discern the authors' intention; they are leery of interpretation, of bias, of spin. This is not always a bad thing. But we also have to unmask presuppositions unique to the post-Enlightenment era, specifically the assumption that "fact" is truth while "fiction" is falsehood or deception.

That being said, we have witnessed in the past decade alone a marked change in our sensibilities.

"The following is based on a true story." Such headings lend credibility to a narrative, whether it's a crime drama, a romance, or an entertaining tale too bizarre to be believed. (Nielsen BookScan reports that nonfiction books outsell fiction by about 100 million books per year.)[3] But while we seem to care very much about whether events actually happened, the lines are increasingly being blurred. The Oscar-winning film *Fargo* (1996) begins with an on-screen message: "This is a true story. The events depicted in this film took place in Minnesota in 1987. At the request of the survivors, the names have been changed. Out of respect for the dead, the rest has been told exactly as it occurred." It turned out,

[2]See Andrew Louth, *Discerning the Mystery: An Essay on the Nature of Theology* (Oxford: Oxford Univ. Press, 1983), chap. 2.

[3]See Lev Grossman, "The Trouble with Memoirs," in *Time* magazine, January 23, 2006.

however, that this was mere playfulness on the part of the writer-directors, who crafted the story entirely out of their own imaginations. Interestingly, this news prompted only a mild degree of indignation from critics and fans.

More recently, news stories revealed that several high-profile memoirs contained material that was made up. In one such case in the news—James Frey's memoir of sin and redemption, *A Million Little Pieces*—many critics were outraged by the revelation that many of the crucial events recounted in the book never actually happened. But, amazingly perhaps, many readers (and even the book's publisher, Random House) defended the book, saying that "a good story is a good story" and that the book has helped countless people confront their addictions.[4]

"Reality television" is another contemporary phenomenon indicative of evolving understandings of fact and fiction. The assumption that such programming depicts reality is almost laughable when we witness the carefully sculpted and strangely predictable emotional scenes, dramatizations, and embellishments of events. Fact and fiction are blurred in this genre, and its immense popularity testifies that we are willing to tolerate such ambiguity in the interest of a good story.

These examples illustrate a few points. On the one hand, we seem to care very much about whether an event actually happened. This is why the tellers of some stories continue to assert, apparently out of a sense of responsibility, that the stories are

[4]See "Call It Fiction," *New York Times*, January 13, 2006, A20; Dan Mitchell, "What Is the Value of Truth?" *New York Times*, January 14, 2006, C5; and Randy Kennedy, "My True Story, More or Less, and Maybe Not at All," *New York Times*, January 15, 2006, "Week in Review," 1.

based on actual events. On the other hand, we retain a respect for story as such, and for both the entertainment and the truth that can be derived from fiction. But we still do not want to be deceived, especially regarding the texts and stories we care about the most. If we are told that a story relates actual events, we expect that to really be the case.

So where does this leave us in our reading of the Holy Bible? A passage from a book on the Old Testament summarizes the modern approach to history and Scripture in the following way:

> Twentieth-century Western audiences are at a major disadvantage when approaching biblical narratives. Our philosophical presuppositions demand that a story produce its historical credentials before it is allowed to speak; we impose modern historical methods on traditional narrative and imagine that our questionable reconstruction of events is more meaningful than the value-laden form in which our community has enshrined its vision. In many of the sciences, we are geniuses when compared to the generations gone by; in the area of traditional narrative, however, we have become unappreciative philistines.[5]

This is summarizes very well where we are in our day. We care about actual events, and at the same time, we don't care. On what does our caring depend? And where does this leave us when we read about the creation of the world and about Adam and Eve in paradise, or for that matter, the rest of Scripture?

[5]Carmel McCarthy and William Riley, *The Old Testament Short Story: Explorations into Narrative Spirituality* (Wilmington, DE: Michael Glazier, 1986), 53.

True Stories

The point of the anecdote that opened this chapter (which, I should hasten to tell you, was based on actual events!) was to show that stories can convey truth independent of whether they actually occurred. We've always known that. Fables, for example, are stories that don't pretend to recount events that happened but which nevertheless speak truth. There may not have ever been a village plagued by a wolf and a mendacious boy, but the idea of "crying wolf" rings true across time and place. Parables come closer to home, since they are among the chief means by which our Lord, according to the Gospels, conveyed the truth about God and his kingdom. Parables speak by way of metaphors, sometimes phrased as similes: "The kingdom of heaven is like a grain of mustard seed . . . " "The kingdom of heaven is like treasure hidden in a field . . . " Other parables are stories: the prodigal son, the publican and the Pharisee. We tell and retell these stories. We read them in the midst of the church. We compose and illustrate children's books about them. They are the subjects of great works of art. The characters come to life for us. They ring true, and so they come to be real for us.

The "reality" of these characters is one of the reasons they can be such potent vehicles for truth. What we find happening in the appreciation of literature in antiquity, as well as in the theological life of the Church, and perhaps especially in the Church's liturgical and prayer life, is that the distinction between historic or "factual" persons and the characters in parables sometimes nearly disappears. In one of the prayers we say in preparation for Holy Communion, for example, there's a line we recite, perhaps without giving it a second thought: "Receive me, O Christ, who loves all, as you received the prostitute, the thief, the publican, and the prodigal."[6] Notice that the first two are people whom the Gospels report as having actually interacted with Christ; the second two are characters from Christ's parables. Similarly, when we prepare for the celebration of Pascha (Easter), we sing cautionary hymns about not becoming like the Pharisee (of the parable), as well as not becoming like Judas (of history). In such cases, their function in our spiritual lives has nothing to do with their historicity; truth is conveyed through story and history alike, story and history together.

Myth

We've looked at fables and parables and seen how the lines between fictive and historical figures can at times be blurred. We need to say something now about myth. *Myth* has been defined in a wide variety of ways. In the earliest classical period, myths were essentially "true stories." But their status as such came to be questioned, even relatively early on. In some of his writing, Plato, for example, didn't seem to like myths very much; he saw them basically as *false* stories, empty tales. (Of course, he wrote his own creation account, the *Timaeus*, largely in the form of a myth, and most of his philosophy is expressed in the form of fictional, constructed dialogues.) From the classical period to the present day, there exist side-by-side both a suspicion of the "mere myth" that isn't true and a welcoming of myths that can be true even if they don't describe actual events.

While the ancients tended not to divide myth from history so acutely (indeed, they conceived these terms quite differently),

---

[6]Communion prayer attributed to St Basil the Great, fourth century.

today most of us consider myths, by their very nature, to be fiction, not describing things that happened in history. But that still leaves us with the question, Is this true fiction or false fiction? On the side of true fiction, myths can be stories, usually set outside of historical time, meant to convey timeless truths—as historian Sallust put it, "A myth never was, but always is."[7] Such myths seek to shed light on reality. Creation myths, especially, and other etiological myths, seek to explain how things came to be as they are, and they do so by way of story. True fiction.

But myth can also denote false fiction. We are today accustomed to speaking of "mere myth," as opposed to fact. In seeking for the truth about a person, we draw the distinction between "the man and the myth." In one sense, this distinction between myth and reality is appropriate, for historicity isn't always beside the point. Some years ago, a friend earnestly told me a story about kidnappers in New York who snatched innocent victims to harvest and sell their organs. We do well to expose this as a mere myth (or an urban legend) rather than a fact. Of course, even the existence of the myth reveals truths about fear in today's big city. But still, it's only a myth, and we needn't fear for our kidneys just yet.

But even when myths convey truth, they aren't meant to be placed side by side with either factual stories or fairy tales; they must speak on their own terms. And when they do, they are liable to speak louder to us and reach deeper into us than prosaic facts can.

[7]Also translated as, "These things never happened, but always are." See "On the Gods and the World," in Gilbert Murray, *Five Stages of Greek Religion* (New York: Doubleday, 1951), 195.

History

So: stories can tell the truth in ways that have little or nothing to do with scientific "historical fact"; such stories aren't lying to anyone even if they don't describe "actual events." This leads us to some final questions about history: What is "historical fact," and what is the relationship between historical events and the written or oral histories that describe them?

There is no unbiased recounting of history: the narration of history takes place from a particular perspective, and usually with a particular end in mind. It is rarely an exercise undertaken for its own sake. More often than not, people write history to shed light on the present, to interpret the present, to explain it, justify it. Written histories can vary a great deal: we can read "historical accounts" of the Communist era in Russia that were written to justify the Leninist-Stalinist ideology; others wrote accounts of the same time and place from a perspective that showed that ideology as having led to state-sponsored barbarism and mass murder.

As to the events themselves that underlie, for example the Russian Communist era, these are gone; they are outside our reach. We only have the accounts—whether of eye-witnesses, social or political historians, commentators—each of which has a perspective. The events matter a great deal: they shaped and continue to shape people's lives. But all that remains are the narratives: people's stories. How these stories are told is everything: the stories can be true, and they can be false.

Stated Intentions

We saw earlier that the importance of the actuality of events can depend on what the audience is being led to believe about them.

So if we read something that is "based on actual events," we feel duped if we find out it was fiction, parable, or myth. Here's where we may want to ask the question, Are the Bible accounts that we've been talking about being passed off as fiction or history?

To answer such a question, we have to bear in mind that the clear-cut distinction between "descriptions of actual events" and "stories about the past" takes on different contours in the pre-modern mind. Fact, embellished fact, and fiction did not dwell in airtight compartments for premoderns; these are *our* categories; they registered differently in the ancient mind.

If we must impose these categories on the scriptural authors, we would find a mixture. They were compiling written and oral material; traditional stories; histories and embellished histories; genealogies and embellished genealogies. As their Christian interpreters, we might add that they were doing all of this under *divine inspiration* (on which we'll say more in a moment).

But as Christians, the question that ought to occupy us is not what the scriptural authors thought. What really matters to us is how *the Church* read and continues to read Scripture. Let's begin by considering some of the earliest and most influential Christian readers of the Old Testament stories. Did they take everything in the Genesis narratives to be historical in a technical or scientific sense? Did they consider its sheer historicity to be of primary, critical importance? Some did and some did not. Let us pose these questions, however anachronistic they may or may not be, to St Paul and the early Church Fathers.

As we approach an answer, one thing is sure: the Scriptures were to them, as to us, holy and inspired, and they engaged them deeply, both as a whole and part-by-part. What would St Paul answer if we were to ask him, "Did Adam and Eve exist 'historically' in the same sense that you and I exist?" Of course it's impossible to know, but he might well say, "Yes," and then immediately say, "But what kind of question is this, anyway?" He might then invite us to read his letter to the Romans, in which he writes clearly about Adam's true function in the larger scale of things. In Romans 5, Paul puts "the one man" Adam at the beginning of sin and death in order to show that "the one man" Christ brings grace, righteousness, and life. Adam's *function*, for St Paul, is to be a "type of the one to come" (Rom 5.14), a prefiguration of Jesus Christ. Adam—as "one man"—functions as the representation of the old dispensation, which is shattered by the coming of Christ. (See also 1 Cor 15.22, 45.) Adam's historical existence is not the point.

Moving onward from St Paul and building on his thought: the historicity question in the early writings of the Church receives a mixed answer, and this fact itself is significant to our inquiry. There was clearly some debate in the early church, although not as sharp and not nearly as prevalent as in our own day, as to how literally one should read the whole Pentateuch, especially the early Genesis narratives. Some of the Fathers said we ought to take the texts at their literal word. St John Chrysostom wrote that we should "believe that a garden came into being in the place that Scripture indicated." In the same sentence, though, he also cautioned against over-literalization, saying, "When you hear that 'God planted a garden in Eden in the east,' take the word 'planted' in a sense appropriate to God—namely that he commanded this to happen."[8]

---

[8]*Homilies on Genesis* 13.13. See Andrew Louth, ed., *Old Testament Vol. 1, Genesis 1–11*, Ancient Christian Commentary on Scripture, vol. 1 (Downers Grove, IL: InterVarsity, 2001), 54.

Other Fathers preferred to leave matters far more open. When St Gregory the Theologian speaks of the creation of the human person, he says, "God placed the human being in paradise, whatever that paradise may have been." He continues, "He placed him there to 'till the plants'—by which it might be meant the Divine Ideas, both simple and complex."[9] In allegorizing or "spiritualizing" the elements of the account, St Gregory draws from one of his beloved teachers, Origen, who was clear in distinguishing between the "spiritual events" and the "historical events" narrated in Scripture. Origen himself, in passages carefully preserved by St Gregory the Theologian and St Basil the Great in their anthology of his writings, rejected the six days of creation as six twenty-four-hour periods, as well as the idea of a literal garden with trees that one could see and feel, whose fruit could be chewed with the teeth, a garden within which God could "walk."[10] And long before theologian Paul Tillich came around to tell us so, St Gregory was saying that Adam's sin depicts an existential reality, that the account of Adam's sin is really about our own ongoing sin: "The weakness of my first father was my own weakness."[11]

However they might have reckoned the question of historicity—and whether they reckoned it at all—the Fathers were united on two fronts. One is that the Genesis narratives have to be interpreted, that we have to come to understand what they really mean

---

[9]*Oration* 38.xii.

[10]This passage from Origen's *On First Principles* IV, which addresses at length the spiritual as well as the historical passages of Scripture, does not factor into the list of "Origenist" heresies that were condemned in the sixth century. It is found in Basil's and Gregory's *Philokalia of Origen*, sections 1–27.

[11]*Oration* 38.xii.

for ourselves and for our salvation. That imperative is all the more evident when the narratives themselves explicitly present us with metaphors: "the tree of life," "the tree of the knowledge of good and evil." All of the Fathers who look back to Genesis work to understand what these things actually mean and the significance and legacy of Adam and Eve's transgressions. The need to interpret the Genesis narratives also comes from the development of cosmology—the understanding of the world in its relation to the universe. Genesis expresses its timeless truth by means of the language and cosmology of its own time, when the earth was conceived of as flat with four corners, supported by pillars, with a firmament separating the waters above from those below. But that cosmology had already been superseded by the patristic era; many of the Fathers—particularly those who were interested in the sciences—adapted the Genesis text in terms of their contemporary understanding of the created world.

The other key factor that unites the Fathers' reading of Genesis is their Christ-centered understanding of it. As we've just seen, the real key to St Paul's interpretation of Adam is Christ, and this christological reading continues as the primary meaning of Genesis. (As we'll see in chapter 5, it is the primary meaning of the entire Old Testament.) Once that perspective is taken—and we could argue that this is the only perspective that truly matters—the question of empirical historicity fades.

Such a diminution of empirical historicity can bring people to the uncomfortable assumption, as it did my Russian friend, that once we deny the historic reality of any biblical account, we're on an inexorable path, a slippery slope, toward denying the historicity of the whole Bible. "If you deny that the flood occurred just as it was written, then you'll deny that Christ rose from the dead, or even that he existed!" This logic assumes that everything we find in the Bible works the same way. It's as if the Bible were one long history book. We customarily regard the Bible as a single book, but it is actually a compilation of books written over centuries in a wide variety of styles and genres with different intentions and functions. We read Genesis 1–3 differently from how we read Proverbs, or the Book of Acts, or the Book of Revelation.

At the same time, we do also read the Bible as a whole, as a single, multifaceted icon. Specifically, it is an icon of Christ. This is what our Lord himself says in the Gospels,[12] and what the Church's patristic and liturgical legacy confirms. This means that our reference point for reading the Bible—and of our "reading" of all of creation—is the central moment of the history of the world: the passion and cross of Christ. This event is the focal point of everything before it or after it, everything that happened and every truth-bearing story that is told. The event itself, which in order to underscore its historical character the Nicene Creed stipulates as having taken place "under Pontius Pilate," is also a manifestation of the timeless reality of Jesus Christ. He is the Lamb who was slain before the foundation of the world (Rev 13.8) but slain also in history in the first century; the one who was "destined before the foundation of the world but was made manifest at the end of the times for your sake" (1 Pet 1.20).

For Orthodox, then, the Old Testament doesn't function as a history book or as a science text. We believe it's a book that exists

[12]Jesus tells his disciples that the Pentateuch (Genesis through Deuteronomy) is about him (Jn 5.46), that the story of Jonah is about him (Mt 12.39–40), and that the whole of the Law, the Psalms, and the Prophets are about him (Lk 24.27, 44).

to point to Christ, to give understanding about who Christ was and what he achieved through his life-giving death. The New Testament, for its part, wasn't written as a cold recitation of uninterpreted events. Merely recording the "historic facts," to the extent that it's possible, wouldn't have been enough to convey the gospel for all to see. The apostles saw everything Jesus did and still didn't understand and internalize the meaning of it all until after he was crucified, when their minds were opened to who he is and how the Scriptures spoke of him. They *then* recounted the events in the Gospels in such a way that reveals Jesus' fulfillment of Old Testament Scripture, his significance for us and for our salvation. The Gospels simultaneously recount and interpret the events of Jesus Christ's life.

In 1 Corinthians 15.3–5, St Paul outlines the primary events that are primary for him, and for us: "For I delivered to you as of first importance what I also received, that Christ died for our sins in accordance with the Scriptures, that he was buried, that he was raised on the third day in accordance with the Scriptures, and that he appeared to Cephas, then to the twelve." Note that even this bare-bones account is an interpretation of the events: Christ died *for our sins* and *in accordance with the Old Testament Scriptures.* It is an interpretation that places the narratives of Scripture at the service of Christ's passion.

There is no slippery slope to reading Scripture this way. There's only an upward slope at whose pinnacle are the cross and the empty tomb.

Inspiration and the "Treasure in Earthen Vessels"

St Paul spoke of the gospel—the good news about Jesus Christ and what God has done through him—as a "treasure in earthen vessels." In chapters 3 and 4 of his Second Epistle to the Corinthians, he characterizes the gospel as something that needs to be unveiled and also unearthed. When we think of Scripture, then, as "inspired by God," we ought to consider both the inspiration of its interpretation and the inspiration of its composition.

But what makes a text inspired? What does it mean that "all Scripture is inspired by God" (2 Tim 3.16)? The amanuensis model (an amanuensis is a scribe, a secretary) has it that Scripture was narrated by God and taken down by the scriptural authors. But the inspiration of Scripture is greater than a dictation exercise; it is the entry of God into human history. It is God's action through the hearts, minds, and hands of the people who wrote things down using the language and imagery of their time, people who compiled oral narratives and liturgical incantations, people who edited previous versions of such compilations. Furthermore, the inspiration didn't stop at the composition and compilation (redaction) of the texts but continues as certain texts were selected over others as authoritative. Inspiration continues, too, in the reading and interpretation of these texts. To suggest that the Genesis creation narratives, for example, are an interweaving of material from a variety of sources (as at least one theory has it) does no disservice to the idea of inspiration. Rather, it makes inspiration into something all the more real, concretely lived out in the complexity of history.

Let's stay with the creation narratives for a moment. Having made these suggestions as to their origin and divine inspiration, let's look at how they work and what they intend to tell us. On the face of it, the Genesis accounts exist to explain the foundation of the world. They show the world to have been established by God, and by God alone, according to his free will, in a deliberate manner and deliberate order, in stages that culminate in the creation of the human person in God's own image and likeness. They explain the human person's relationship to God, to the created world, and to other persons. They explain both the origin and perpetuation of evil, sin, and tragedy in the world. They establish the tribe that would become God's chosen people, from whom would rise the Savior of the world.

As we saw earlier, when we read the New Testament, the Fathers, and the liturgy, we see that the Genesis accounts exist not only to establish these basics but also to point to the Truth himself; they prefigure Christ. Adam is "a type of the one to come" (Rom 5.14). He is the old man; Christ is the new man. Eve, the mother of all living, who disobeyed God, is a type of the Church, personified in Mary, the mother of the one who is life, and who said to God, "Let it be to me according to your will." The tree of life in the garden is a type of the cross. The garden itself is a type of the Church and of the New Jerusalem. This is what we sing in the Church throughout the year. All that is given to us in the Genesis accounts, together with the truth they convey about our origin, is a shadow of the reality that awaits its fulfillment in Christ.

When we say that the writing of the Genesis narratives was inspired by God, and that the narratives are *true,* it does not necessarily follow that God was dictating a chronicle of historic events that could be placed in a manner contiguous with recorded human history. The truth of Genesis lies in the divine inspiration of its composition and in the divine inspiration of its interpretation in the Church. This dimension of its fulfillment in Christ is why, among all of the other creation stories that exist (some with remarkable parallels to Genesis, and some strikingly different), we know Genesis to be uniquely true. It is for us *the* creation story, even if, by God's grace and by the presence of his Word, the other stories, whether they originate before or after the composition of the Genesis accounts, may sometimes reflect or resonate with them.

I began by trying to show the truth-telling capacity of myth, story, and history. I'd like now to explore further the ways in which truth is conveyed through story, looking at some of the stories and myths among us today.

The Story Continues

The Gospel according to Harry Potter. The Gospel according to Tolkien. The Gospel Reloaded. Holy Superheroes: Exploring Faith and Spirituality in Comic Books. These are titles of just a few of the hundreds of books, all published in the last five years, which testify to an increasing desire to find the truth—specifically the Christian truth—that wittingly or unwittingly underlies some contemporary stories and myths.

Christian allegories, or the allegorizing of theological and moral themes, is by no means new to anyone who knows Dante or John Bunyan. But there are also the myths of the world, whether ancient or modern, which seem to reflect the Christian story—gods that take the form of humans, virgin births, floods, sacrificial deaths and rebirths. The idea of universal elements in mythologies has been explored by Carl Jung and popularized by Joseph Campbell and his disciples. Their theories, particularly as they point to a collective subconscious, are full of insight, but to a Christian perspective, they require an adjustment, or a reorientation, to be fulfilled: *Christ* is the way, the truth, and the life, the Logos, the one in whom all things, and all true myths, hold together.

It has been said that the overwhelming popularity of J. R. R. Tolkien's Lord of the Rings trilogy, C. S. Lewis' Narnia stories, and the Harry Potter phenomenon has to do with the fact that, intentionally or not, they resonate deeply with the one true story, the story of the Son of God who was made man for us and for our salvation, lifted up on the cross of his own accord, and raised from the dead. Lewis himself often makes the point that stories and myths, both in the Bible as well as outside it, bear truth insofar as they resonate with this true story.[13] An advocate of this theory is John Granger, an Orthodox Christian who was so struck by the Christian message woven deeply into the Harry Potter novels that he wrote two vivid and literate books on the subject.[14]

Granger has read Lewis and Tolkien closely. Not only are most of their mythical stories built on the bedrock of Christian imagery and theology, but their essays and letters constantly come back to the same point: underlying any good myth, whenever and wherever it was told, lies the one, true, historical myth of Christianity. The popularity of such stories, especially when

[13]See, for example, C. S. Lewis, *The Pilgrim's Regress* (Grand Rapids, MI: Eerdmans, 1958), 154; 171.

[14]*The Hidden Key to Harry Potter: Understanding the Meaning, Genius, and Popularity of Joanne Rowling's Harry Potter Novels* (Port Hadlock, WA: Zossima, 2002), and *Looking for God in Harry Potter* (Wheaton, IL: Tyndale, 2004).

they are crafted creatively, owes to our natural resonance with Jesus Christ and with the story of his incarnation, life, death, and resurrection. Granger usefully summarizes, "As images of God designed for life in Christ, all humans naturally resonate with stories that reflect the greatest story ever told—the story of God who became man."[15]

Star Wars is another epic creation that draws on a variety of religious expressions. Star Wars can be said to resonate with Christian truth in part owing to its depiction of the battle between good and evil, both between different characters and within particular characters. Alongside this universal and potent drama are passing resonances with Christianity in what we might call the "wisdom literature" of Star Wars, emanating from Yoda or other high-ranking Jedi—wisdom that could also be claimed by numerous religious traditions.[16] It's stock wisdom, much of it true and some of it banal. And of course there's also a lot of very mixed-up imagery thrown in. But it's hard not to read Christ into Obi-Wan's voluntary and life-giving death in episode 4.

Indeed, the Jesus story continues to compel modern filmmakers. Some depict it literally (Mel Gibson's *The Passion of the Christ*) and others metaphorically (Denys Arcand's *Jesus of Montreal*). But a great number of adventure, science fiction, and superhero stories and films incorporate Christ imagery and feature characters who can properly be seen as Christ figures, whether it's the cowboy who comes from some unknown place to rid a town of its evil, or the displaced Babette, whose presence transfigures a

[15]Granger, *Looking for God in Harry Potter*, xix.

[16]See Dick Staub, *Christian Wisdom of the Jedi Masters* (San Francisco: Jossey-Bass, 2005).

Danish village in *Babette's Feast*. In modern films, there are countless voluntary and life-giving deaths, often accompanied by quite
unconcealed cross or crucifix imagery. Watch the last scenes of
The Matrix: Revolutions, in which Neo, in becoming himself a
curse, defeats the evil one by filling him with light, only to be lifted
up in glory with his arms outstretched cruciform, after which the
good news of victory is proclaimed to Zion. Watch the scene in
Spiderman 2 in which the superhero, his arms outstretched, saves
the multitudes on the subway train and in so doing shows them
his true identity and awakens their communion with one another
and with him. These scenes take place in contexts that are full of
other, patently non-Christian imagery too. They are not the
gospel, and they don't pretend to be. But it may just be that the
truth of Christ speaks through key episodes in these stories,
whether or not the authors intended it.

Is this merely a pious "eisegesis?" In other words, are we merely
reading Christian truth into this output? Is Christianity in the eye
of the beholder? These are appropriate questions, especially when
we consider that the authors of many of these stories do not profess any intention of depicting Christian reality. Yet finding Christ
and the cross in these ways has a solid history. It is reminiscent of
Justin Martyr, who saw the cross everywhere—in things made by
human hands, like ship masts and tools, and in the things of
nature, like the human face.[17] This is the same Justin who claimed
the truth, wherever it was found, as *Christian* truth.

When St Paul preached at the Areopagus (Acts 17.16–34), he
cited pagan scriptures and alluded to pagan statues, showing how
they point to God, the Father of Jesus Christ. Many of today's

[17]*First Apology*, 55.

cultural symbols are liable to point to Christ as well. They can't help it, because the Truth that underlies everything simply bursts through.

Truth, story, myth, history, allegory, typology: what do these all mean? Can't we just read our Bible *simply*? Maybe we should all just spend more of our time with the kinds of people who are utterly untouched by these categories and questions. Yet the times in which we live demand the kind of inquiry I've been sketching here. We live in an age when the categories of truth, fiction, and myth are both clearer and more muddled than ever. We are obsessed with finding "the truth behind the myth," and yet, the Lord of the Rings trilogy notwithstanding, we've nearly lost the meaning and effect of myth. In our age, too, debates about creation and evolution, or creation as evolution, rage in the public square, and fundamentalist readings of Scripture are gaining in popularity. We owe it to ourselves to bring to the fore questions about the nature and function of story. These questions can be a part of our maturing into a faith that penetrates the whole of our being.

part two

DISCERNING DOGMA

chapter four
KNOWING THE UNKNOWABLE: IS THEOLOGY POSSIBLE?

Mystery and Mind

The truth about God, to which the Spirit is leading us, is awesome. More than that, it's incomprehensible. The Bible teaches that God is unknowable in his essence: God's unknowability is one of his inherent characteristics. If we think about it, it's impossible to know *anyone* fully, to their core, in such a way that nothing will ever surprise us about them. It's impossible even to know ourselves. So when it comes to knowing the God who is above and beyond everything that exists, and who brought everything into being out of nothing, we are talking about a radical unknowability. No one and nothing has created God: he simply is. This is why the name he reveals to Moses is nothing more and nothing less than "I AM" (Ex 3.14).

We humans, along with the rest of the universe, are created. The difference between created and uncreated is an unbridgeable chasm, making God radically other than the universe and anything in it. All of this hammers home the point: we know *who* God is—the

God of Abraham, Isaac, and Jacob, the Father of Jesus Christ—but we will never know *what* God is, for he is beyond knowledge, beyond expression.

When it comes to understanding God, two theological questions have occupied, or perhaps haunted, Christian minds since the first century. One concerns Jesus Christ and how this one person can at the same time be completely divine, in every way the same as God, "true God from true God," but also completely human, in every essential way the same as you and me, flesh and bone, susceptible to fatigue and hunger and death. How can this be? You can't be two contradictory things at once, especially when they are bridging the unbridgeable chasm. The second question concerns the Trinity. Ever since we have come to know Jesus Christ, who calls himself the unique Son of the Father, who says he is one with the Father, and who also speaks of the Holy Spirit, the Lord, we reckon three who are divine, yet we worship one God. How is this possible?

I raise this point to emphasize that not only is God inherently unknowable but, even in his complete revelation to us in his Son, he presents our minds with paradoxes that we can neither fully grasp nor fully express. Our minds are limited. Our words are limited. God is limitless and other than us. The task is daunting.

And yet, just when we are about to pack our theological bags and abandon the project, we need to recall that God created us in his image. Furthermore, he gave us minds, and he reveals himself to us.

Let's look briefly at each of these three facts.

We are made in God's image. It's not the other way around. This means that anything we say about God, such as "He is good," or even "He exists," has to be understood properly, that is, the right way around. We can't assume that what we understand as "existence" (such as the existence of trees and rocks, or ourselves) is the same for the God who says "I AM." We can't be reading what we understand as "good" or "loving" or "wise" into God either. But God's existence, goodness, love, and wisdom, while at the same time radically other, are the archetypes of created existence, goodness, love, and wisdom. We can speak of God because we bear his image, but we have to be conscious of the "direction" of our speech: we are made in God's image, not the other way around.

But back to basics, our being made in God's image means that, even if God is radically other than us, we are also quite profoundly related to him. This, we say, is why a relationship with God in Christ is so organic to our very being. A Christian believes that the true home of every human being is in God, the God of Jesus. It means, too, that we can go a long way toward knowing God by knowing ourselves and by knowing the created world, since it is an expression of God's being (Rom 1.20). The Church's ascetical writers consistently teach that the contemplation of nature is a way of coming into communion with God and into knowledge of God.

While the whole of our being—body, soul, mind, spirit—is in God's image, one aspect of us is truly unique to ourselves as human beings: our mind. Plants and animals share with us a physical, bodily being, as well as a kind of life force. Animals share even more with us: they have souls in the sense of having perception, instinct, and the emotions of fear and anger, and perhaps more than that. But humans alone have a rational mind, which the New Testament and the Greek church authors called the *nous*. That word is difficult to render in English; most translators use the word *mind* or *intellect*, sometimes even using the word *spirit*. The difficulty comes because, for us today, the words *mind* or *intellect* or *rationality* connote something of cold calculation. We think of intellectual as opposed to creative, mind as opposed to heart, rational as opposed (perhaps) to vibrant or free. The *nous*, that faculty that humans alone possess,[1] encompasses all of these qualities holistically: intellectual, spiritual, creative, rational, free.

In the Church we understand this mind of ours, this free, and creative intellect, to have been given us by God as an instrument to help us come to know him and to share in his life. As you can see, the word *nous* is therefore important for us to understand: it is a key to understanding human nature and to justifying the whole enterprise of theology. It allows us to try to express with human words and human concepts things that are inexpressible, because we believe that we've been given the faculty, and therefore the responsibility, to do so. We acknowledge the limitations of our reasoning capabilities, and we are called to transform and renew our minds. But at the same time, we are supposed to *use* our minds, to think, to reason about both divine and created things. Doing so properly, in prayer and in communion and council with others, is an act of genuine reverence to God.

Finally, we believe that the unknowable God reveals himself to us, through Christ and by his Holy Spirit. Citing St Paul once again: "What no eye has seen, nor ear heard, nor the heart of man conceived, what God has prepared for those who love him, God has

---

[1]Exception: an angel is a "nous," though without a body.

revealed to us through the Spirit." He continues, "For the Spirit searches everything, even the depths of God" (1 Cor 2.9–10).

God reveals himself to us in what the Church Fathers called his *energies*. Here is another word we need to dissociate from its sheerly physical sense, because these energies aren't physical emanations. God reveals himself through and in his creation. He acts in history, is involved with created things; he is *in* everything that exists. The Fathers spoke interchangeably of God's energies, operations, and actions.

God's self-revelation in his energies is not a partial revelation. It's not like you and me, who reveal ourselves only partially and imperfectly to each other, behind facades we create. God is simple. This is one of the basic and most profound teachings about him: his perfect simplicity means that his revelation to us in his energies is truly a revelation of who and what he is. This revelation is most evident and clear in the person of Jesus Christ, and nowhere more so than in Jesus' voluntary death for us on the cross.

All of this is to say: although God is an unknowable mystery and we shall never know him in his essence; although we are limited, created beings with limited words and limited capacities for understanding; although we are fallen and prone to distorted vision; we know that we are made in God's image, we trust that we are being led to the truth by the Holy Spirit, and we know that God reveals himself to us in his energies. And so we can go a long way in expressing things about him which we believe to be true. We trust, too, that our very lives and salvation are bound up with searching for and coming to know these things, insofar as they bring us into communion with God himself.

We mustn't forget that our words about God, which are often technical and may be terms and categories inherited from Greek, Latin, or Syriac philosophy and modes of thinking, ought finally to be about glorifying him. They should be words of love and praise. The very awesomeness of the task of theology should not prevent us from entering that task, but its awesomeness should always be before us. As St Cyril of Jerusalem wrote:

> If someone will say that the essence of God is incomprehensible, then why do we speak about him? Well, is it really true that just because I cannot drink the whole river I will not take water from it in moderation for my benefit? . . . Or for that matter, because I have entered into a great garden and cannot eat all the supply of fruits, would you have me go away altogether hungry? . . . I am attempting now to glorify the Lord, not to describe him, knowing nevertheless that I shall fall short of glorifying him worthily. Still I deem it a work of piety even to attempt it at all.[2]

Why Do Theology?

If we have established that theology is possible, we haven't yet discussed why we ought to bother with it. After all, it's not only complex, it's often contentious. It seems to divide Christians more than unite them. So shouldn't we be a lot simpler about these things, which are ultimately beyond our grasp anyway?

The short answer to that question is that, in every age, people get it wrong. From the first century to the twenty-first, some people

[2]*Catechetical Lectures* VI.5.

who call themselves Christians teach that Jesus Christ was a kind of spiritual phantom, that he didn't live a human life. And some say that he was merely a good human being who had a special relationship with God. And still others say that God is one person who reveals himself in three different modes—sometimes as Father, sometimes as Son, and sometimes as Holy Spirit. Such views cannot coexist with the teachings reached within the Orthodox Church. The Church's teachings, as we will see in the next chapter, were often worked out precisely because such alternate views arose. These heresies served as catalysts or necessitators of orthodox theology.

Theology isn't just a defense against heresy, however, even if the heresy might have helped to elicit it. Theology enriches our lives. Theology enriches our praise of God. Etymologically, that's what *orthodoxy* means: the *right* (ortho) *praise* (doxia) of God. We believe our theology to be the truth, that salvation is bound up with knowledge of the truth. We owe it to ourselves to know whatever we can about God, his Christ, his Spirit, and his creation. St Vincent of Lérins put it well:

> After all, what the councils have proclaimed in their decrees was nothing other than that which before was believed plainly and simply, brought forth so that it might from now on be believed more diligently. . . . Aroused by the novelties of the heretics, again and again the catholic church has, by the authoritative decrees of its councils, handed down to posterity what it earlier received from our forebears by tradition alone, condensing weighty matters in a few words and, particularly for

the enlightenment of the mind, presenting in new words the old interpretation of the faith.[3]

The purpose of our continued theological reflection and refinement is, as Vincent says, to believe "more diligently," to continue to hand down what we have received, and to do so in ways and with words that speak to people in their own times and places.

Checks and Balances: Asceticism and Conciliarity

Our justification for the task of theology has a hugely important qualification. True, God reveals himself, and he created us in his image and endowed us with a mind to engage his self-revelation. But we are lost if we fail to remember that our minds are imperfect. Not only are they inherently limited in ability to perceive, to process, and to express, but they are also (for want of a better word) fallen. The Genesis creation narratives teach us that, through our freely willed decisions, we turn away from God. Our desire for short-term gratification—money, power, sex, or pleasure—clouds our thinking. We sin. We misdirect the orientation of our whole lives. This situation, which is systemic in a way, means that the image or icon of God is distorted in us. So the very mechanism by which we are supposed to reason about the world, about ourselves, and about God is prone to malfunction.

At the same time, the Orthodox Church rejects the idea that the human person is totally depraved, that God's image is obliterated

---

[3]*The Commonitories*, chap. 23. (See *Niceta of Remesiana, Sulpicius Severus, Vincent of Lerins, Prosper of Aquitaine,* trans. Gerald G. Walsh, et al., The Fathers of the Church, vol. 7 (New York, 1949), 312, translation altered. I am grateful to Jim Payton for directing me to this quotation.

in us. No. Human nature is good and naturally tends toward God, though that tendency gets distorted, misdirected. We can cooperate in God's action to redirect us to what we truly are: his image-bearing creation. This means that the task and responsibility of theology, of the Spirit-led pursuit of the truth, entail two critical factors, one dealing with our own individual selves, the other having to do with ourselves in communion with each other. They are asceticism and conciliarity, two more words that require some unpacking.

Asceticism

Asceticism isn't only about hair shirts and vows; neither is it the exclusive task of the people called to a monastic way of life. Asceticism is work toward purity and virtue; it is the task of all Christians, of anyone who wants to think and live truly. We are holistic beings, and the pursuit of right-mindedness or whole-mindedness (as in the Greek *sophrosyne* or the Russian *tselomudrie*) involves our whole being. Asceticism is the redirection of our selves toward God, in our minds and bodies. Though we believe that the human person is created good—in body, soul, and mind—and remains inherently good despite the distortions, we need to be in the business of overcoming the distortions and finding our true selves. It's not for nothing that we say that people who are sane, composed, and thinking properly are "in their right mind," while people who are thinking in a distorted way are "out of their mind." Asceticism is, among other things, the striving ever to be in our right mind.

The distortions I keep talking about have to do with the passions. The passions are what Christians (and also Greek philosophers and other thinkers) narrow down to the basic faculties of zeal and desire. Properly oriented, these become a passionate zeal and desire for God, truth, communion with each other in Christ, everything that is truly good and beautiful. When the passions are turned the wrong way, zeal becomes anger, bitterness, pride, despair. Desire becomes the lust for pleasure and power. Doesn't this ring true when we look at ourselves?

Throughout the history of Christian writing, the way to overcoming or redirecting passions is linked with learning the truth by the Holy Spirit. St Paul sets it out plainly to the Galatians: "But I say, walk by the Spirit, and do not gratify the desires of the flesh. For the desires of the flesh are against the Spirit, and the desires of the Spirit are against the flesh; for these are opposed to each other, to prevent you from doing what you would" (5.16–17). He lists pursuits that are incompatible with walking by the Spirit: fornication, impurity, licentiousness, idolatry, sorcery, enmity, strife, jealousy, anger, selfishness, dissension, envy, and drunkenness (vv. 19–21). On the other hand, "the fruit of the Spirit is love, joy, peace, patience, kindness, goodness, faithfulness, gentleness, self-control" (vv. 21–22). He sums up: "Those who belong to Christ Jesus have crucified the flesh with its passions and desires. If we live by the Spirit, let us also walk by the Spirit" (vv. 24–25).

Crucifying our flesh to walk by the Spirit and be led by the Spirit sounds radical, and it is. But it's not the physical flesh itself that is to be brought into submission, rather "its passions and desires." Asceticism is the checking, restraint, and redirection of our desires, compulsions, habits, addictions, and impulses. It takes many forms, depending on who we are and the context of our lives, but it will generally involve degrees of self-restraint in matters of food and drink, sexual expression, entertainment, acquisition, and other kinds of gratification and stimulation. All of these are good things when used properly, but they are also awfully prone to abuse.

In cases where the misdirection of our passions has gone far, and in cases of genuine addiction and compulsion, self-restraint can be a superhuman effort, sometimes best undertaken with professional guidance and/or the help of a twelve-step program. The road to recovery can really feel like a crucifixion of the flesh. But in less extreme cases as well, our use of the things of the world and our care for our bodily needs and desires must be exercised consciously and continuously. There is a kind of asceticism that we undertake only periodically, such as when we give up certain activities during fasting periods; otherwise, it's a constant thing for us as we restrain ourselves from speaking an extra word of gossip or anger, hold back from a third cup of coffee, refrain from indulging in a lustful glance. Again, depending on our character and our situation, it will look different for different people. The ways we apply asceticism are best decided with the assistance of a spiritual guide who knows us: we are not on this road alone. And sometimes we are not the best judges of ourselves. The way of purity, like the way of theology, as we shall see, is both a personal and a communal enterprise.

Until now, I've mentioned only the negatives of asceticism, the restraints and checks. The positives are many: they involve an engagement with the life of the Church. That means an ongoing participation in the sacramental life, especially sacramental confession and Holy Communion, regular and attentive attendance at the church services, regular reading of Scripture, and regular prayer. Asceticism also involves what St Paul calls a meditation or thinking on "whatever is true, whatever is honorable, whatever is just, whatever is pure, whatever is lovely, whatever is gracious . . . any excellence . . . anything worthy of praise" (Phil 4.8). This is the right "input," which helps direct our response to the stimuli of our daily lives—all the words, images, sounds.

This is a way of reshaping the distorted image in us and recovering the God-given mind-heart that seeks the truth through the guidance of the Holy Spirit. So we're back to a point made in chapter 1: seeking the truth and living rightly are inextricably bound to each other. The Church Fathers constantly repeat, "This is the knowledge of God: the keeping of God's commandments."[4] The pursuit of theological truth entails living purely, or more precisely put, being *on the road to purity*, for one never arrives at purity of mind-heart or achieves it in a final way. Being on the way is all that is asked.

The pursuit of the truth, the discussion of theology, has certain preconditions, writes St Gregory the Theologian. Alluding to Psalm 46.11, he says that "we need actually to 'be still' in order to know God." The study and discussion of theology "is not for all, but only for those who have been tested and have found a sound footing in study and contemplation, and, more importantly, have undergone, or at the very least are undergoing, purification of body and soul."[5] St John of the Ladder agrees: "It is dangerous to swim when fully dressed, and it is dangerous, when carried away by passions, to investigate the mysteries of

[4]Basil the Great, *Homily* 337.iv.

[5]*Oration* 27.iii; iv

the Godhead."[6] We are familiar with another way of putting it: "Blessed are the pure in heart, for they shall see God" (Mt 5.8).

Conciliarity

Another factor in the pursuit of theology is conciliarity (from the word *council*), not only because we believe in *communion* as our natural state of being but also because of the hazards of reasoning alone, in isolation from others. Certainly much of our thinking, reasoning, and studying takes place privately, as does our personal prayer. But that can't be the only reasoning, nor can it be the only kind of prayer. We also have a prayer life that is corporate, in the Church. Our study of the Scriptures, the liturgy, and the Church Fathers brings us into council with others, with Christ's holy Church.

The ancient adage *unus Christianus, nullus Christianus* ("one Christian, no Christian") means that a Christian doesn't exist in isolation. The Church is defined by conciliarity, to the extent that we could even say that the Church is a great council or communion of persons who have lived throughout history and throughout the world. It is about human beings in community with each other and with Christ.

Conciliarity is, to put it minimally, give and take with others; maximally, it is communion with Christ in and through the Church. We may think of conciliarity both historically and geographically, for one dimension of conciliarity is a communion with history. Our

[6]*The Ladder of Divine Ascent*, trans. Colm Luibheid and Norman Russell, Classics of Western Spirituality (Mahwah, NJ: Paulist, 1982), step 27, p. 262.

pursuit of the truth about God is done in council with Scripture and with those who reasoned together in history, whose reasoning is seen by the Church as right and true. Isaac Newton famously said, "If I have seen further, it is by standing on the shoulders of giants." We study those who lived and wrote in the past in order to benefit from their collective wisdom. But our pursuit of the truth is also done in council with others alive today, wherever they may be located. We discuss our theological reflection with each other, checking it with each other and with each other's understanding of the Church's tradition.

Conciliarity functions as a kind of checks-and-balances system. We know that our individual thinking, and even to an extent our corporate thinking, is subject to error and even to delusion, and therefore we submit our thinking to the council of the Church. But conciliarity isn't a matter only of checking up on one another. Theology is by nature a communal enterprise, because human personhood is founded on communion.

I don't wish to lose track of our basic theme here, which is the necessity for conciliarity in the pursuit of true theology, but the theme of conciliarity invites a brief reflection on one of the basic dynamics of the Church, both in its teachings and in its ministry and ordering. I am speaking of the dynamic of *conciliar hierarchy*, or *hierarchical conciliarity.*

Hierarchy is another concept, like dogma and authority, that makes people bristle. Conciliar hierarchy sounds like an oxymoron, a pairing of ideas that negate each other. In common parlance, hierarchy sounds like a top-down structure, a triangle, or maybe a ladder in which someone has authority and privilege over anyone who stands on a rung below them. We ought to recover an earlier, more neutral usage of this term; a hierarchy is any kind of order or structure which gives shape to a process and enables it to move along its appointed flow.

Because we are systemically prone to the lust for power, hierarchy is subject to abuse; a certain suspicion of it is justified. But we shouldn't be paralyzed by the term. We must be guided by our Lord's own words, repeated in all three of the Synoptic Gospels (Matthew, Mark, and Luke). When the disciples ask him who is the greatest, he warns them about wrong approaches to authority, in which people "lord it over" each other. He teaches the authority of service and humility, and he puts it to the proof by spreading out his hands and dying for the people over whom he is Lord. We look also to Ephesians 5, where St Paul balances a wife's obedience to her husband with the husband's self-giving love and self-sacrifice unto death. The master is servant: that is how hierarchy ought to operate.

Genuine authority is never a one-way street, never a dictation without listening. And so genuine hierarchy is conciliar hierarchy, modeled on the life of the Holy Trinity itself. The Father is the source of the Son and of the Spirit, and so in a sense is greater than the Son and the Spirit (Jn 14.28). Yet the Father is of one essence and of one mind with his Son and Spirit. The actions of God are never the actions of the Spirit alone, or the Son alone, or even the Father alone.

The Orthodox Church is a hierarchical church. There are clear lines of authority working from the local to the universal level; there are levels of primacy among bishops and among their respective sees. And the bishop does have authority: he judges how canons are applied for the salvation of souls. But although a bishop is by vocation a keeper and teacher of the apostolic faith, no single bishop, even if he is patriarch, has the authority to put forward a new teaching on his own authority. On theological matters—and on key disciplinary and structural matters—the bishop can't act alone. The canons forbid it. As St Cyprian of Carthage said, *episcopatus unus est*: the episcopate is one, and the bishops hold the episcopate as owners of a common property. Furthermore, perhaps especially in our own day, the authoritative voice of the bishops on all matters—ecclesiastical, canonical, bioethical, theological, moral—relies on the consultative work of commissions and persons (lay or ordained) who are qualified to reflect on these things.

Authority (including theological authority) rests, therefore, in the conciliar dimension of the Church. Councils may be run hierarchically—convened by the authorities and constituted largely of bishops—but they are *councils*, meaning that they represent the mind of the whole assembly. Furthermore—and this is key—councils themselves are not authoritative unless they have been accepted (or "received") by the wider conciliarity of the Church. Some councils in church history, though summoned by all the appropriate entities, were not accepted by the Church as a whole and ended up carrying no authority whatsoever.

Conciliar hierarchy: both poles are vital. Hierarchy, because without authority and structure there would be no forward motion; conciliarity, because one-sided authority leads too easily to despotism and abuse. Or as Fr Thomas Hopko has put it, hierarchy without conciliarity is tyranny. Conciliarity without hierarchy is anarchy.[7]

---

[7]See "Theological Education and Modernity," in *Speaking the Truth in Love:*

We will reflect more on these key principles later in this book. But for the time being, we ought to bear in mind that the pursuit of theology—the pursuit of knowing the unknowable—must be done by people who are striving to live and think rightly, seeking also to live and think in communion with the Church, that great council which is Christ's own body.

Education, Mission, and Witness in Contemporary Orthodoxy (Crestwood, NY: St Vladimir's Seminary Press, 2004), 33. See also Alexander Schmemann, "Towards a Theology of Councils," in *Church, World, Mission: Reflections on Orthodoxy in the West* (Crestwood, NY: St Vladimir's Seminary Press, 1979), chap. 8.

chapter five

"THE SPIRIT WILL GUIDE YOU INTO ALL TRUTH": THE MECHANICS OF DOCTRINE

W e've noticed a few consistent connections in what Scripture says about truth. One is the link between truth and action. The Scriptures say that truth is inextricably related to ethics—what we do, how we act. This relationship involves a circle of two cause-and-effect relationships: (1) if you want to know the truth, you have to act rightly, you have to live in a right way, and (2) to the extent you do know the truth, it's pointless if it doesn't lead you to an ever-increasingly right way of life. Knowing the truth isn't an end in itself.

The other connection we explored in far greater depth is the connection between truth and Christ. Jesus Christ, by whom the world was created, is the perfect expression of God's being. He is called God's Son, of the same being or essence as the Father. The prose and the prayers of the Church also call Jesus "God's Truth," "God's Wisdom," "God's Peace," "God's Power." Having shown us God in the flesh, Jesus Christ reveals, as no other does, the truth. The truth describes what he is.

Finally, we saw briefly the way Scripture links truth and the Holy Spirit. The Spirit of truth (Jn 14.17; 15.26), the Spirit who *is* the truth (1 Jn 5.6), guides us into all truth by leading to Jesus, by showing us who Jesus is, the Son of God.

These different connections are also themselves interwoven. Scriptural passages interlink truth, ethics, the Spirit, and Christ. Reading St John's gospel (chaps. 14–16), we find Jesus entwining at least three strands:

1. His exhortation to love and do his commandments;

2. his promise of the Spirit, who will guide into all truth;

3. his promise that the Spirit will bear witness to him, glorifying him, and reminding the disciples of what Jesus said and did.

The last two strands will occupy our attention in this chapter. How does the Spirit take up where Christ left off in his earthly ministry? Christ taught by his words and also most profoundly by "the word of his cross" (1 Cor 1.18). The end of St Luke's gospel also records how, in his resurrected form, Christ showed the disciples how to understand the Scriptures (the law, the prophets, and the psalms) in terms of himself, and how to make sense of his earthly life and death. But after he was gone from among them, the disciples didn't merely rely on their personal, creative analysis of their memories of him. The Spirit guided them into truth. How?

Here are the kinds of questions we'll be exploring:

* What is meant by the promise that the Spirit will come to guide us?

* What is the truth that would be revealed, and to whom would it be revealed?

* How did the Church's teaching come to be formulated? And how do we discern which teachings are indeed true and guided by the Holy Spirit?

These are important questions because we believe that the Church is that society within which the truth is taught. We believe that the teachings of the Church are true, that they are inspired by the Holy Spirit. The problem is, of course, that anyone can say that he or she was guided by the Holy Spirit to some belief or action. The Holy Spirit, as we know from Scripture, "blows where it wills" (Jn 3.8). The Holy Spirit is beyond our grasp, which makes claiming guidance from the Spirit all the more awesome—but also all the more open to misuse. It is an awesome thing that a person, even a church, can be led by the Holy Spirit. We ought to be struck by the terror of such a claim: when we make it for our Orthodox Church, we have to be able to back it up.

The Descent of the Holy Spirit

The first Christians clearly believed that the Spirit had been sent to them exactly as God had promised through the prophets (Joel 2.28–29) and Jesus. Christ's departure brought the descent of the Holy Spirit, as testified dramatically by the Pentecost account recorded in Acts 2. The disciples knew that the Spirit guided them into the truth about everything that really matters: even as the Pentecost event was still under way, Peter found himself able to preach the truth, in his case about Joel's and Jesus' words of promise about the Spirit. He preached Christ with such power that his listeners were "cut to the heart" (Acts 2.37). From then on, the disciples' understanding and preaching was transformed, illumined.

St Paul came onto the scene after Pentecost. But he knew full well how he and his fellow preachers were able to communicate the wisdom of God: it was by the Holy Spirit. In his First Letter to the Corinthians, he writes that in preaching the crucified Christ, he is imparting a wisdom that "no eye has seen, nor ear heard, nor the heart of man conceived." These things, he says, "God has revealed to us through the Spirit" (1 Cor 2.9–10). "Now," continues Paul, "we have received not the spirit of the world, but the Spirit which is from God, so that we might understand the gifts bestowed on us by God. And we impart this in words not taught by human wisdom but taught by the Spirit" (vv. 12–13).

Similarly, in Ephesians (1.13–14) he says, "In Christ, you also, who have heard the word of truth, the gospel of your salvation, and have believed in him, were sealed with the promised Holy Spirit, which is the guarantee of our inheritance."

He follows with a lengthy prayer that the Spirit of wisdom would illumine the hearts of believers, so that they may know God's immeasurable power as accomplished in Christ for the Church, which is Christ's own body (vv. 15–23). This rich passage again associates the Spirit with truth, with wisdom, and with the continuity of a right understanding about Christ.

The Holy Spirit is thoroughly and consistently associated with the guarantee of the inheritance, the continued understanding of truth after Christ's ascension. As Paul writes to his fellow minister Timothy, "Guard the truth [literally, the *paratheke,* or "good deposit"] that has been entrusted to you by the Holy Spirit who dwells within us" (2 Tim 1.14). So it is that the disciples, having been given the Holy Spirit, felt empowered to discern and preach the truth.

And that truth, as I've repeated, is Jesus Christ. He is the one by whom we know God and the mystery of God's will; he is the one in whom all things hold together. And he is the one to whom the Spirit leads us. As soon as Jesus says that the Spirit will "guide you into all the truth," he explains that the Spirit "will glorify *me*" (Jn 16.13–14). It's by the Spirit alone that we understand who Jesus is; we don't know him as Lord, as divine, except by the Spirit (1 Cor 12.3).

The next question is, Whom is the Spirit guiding into all truth? Jesus is talking to his apostles, after all, when he promises the guidance and the comfort of the Holy Spirit. And the scriptural account of Pentecost describes the apostles as recipients of the Spirit, who rested on their heads like fiery tongues. So is it only the apostles who are being guided to all truth, to Christ?

In a manner of speaking, yes, it is the apostles. The two main hymns sung on the Feast of Pentecost, when we celebrate the descent of the Holy Spirit, are instructive. They show the effect of the Spirit on the apostles (fishermen), then on everyone else:

> Blessed are you, O Christ our God,
> Who has revealed the fishermen to be the wisest of all
> By sending down on them the Holy Spirit.
> Through them you have drawn the whole world into
> your net!

The second contrasts the divisive confusion at the tower of Babel, where no one could understand anyone else, with the unity that emerged at Pentecost:

> When the Most High came down and confused the
>   tongues, he divided the nations,
> But when he distributed the tongues of fire, he called all
>   to unity.

Pentecost, though a particular event, has universal implications. Not just the apostles but *all* are called to unity. How? The first hymn explains it: it is *through* the apostles that we are all incorporated into the Pentecost event. This is where the Church comes in: the Spirit guides into truth through that society which is founded on the apostles. This is one of the reasons we call the Church "apostolic": it is the Church inaugurated by Christ and the Spirit through the apostles.[1] It is also why we call our faith apostolic; although it is necessarily expressed in each age in different languages and forms, it's the same faith that was preached by the apostles.

When the Church celebrates the apostles, we sing that "their proclamation has gone out into all the world, and their words to the ends of the universe." Like the starry heavens which tell of God's glory, the apostles preach the Spirit-given faith of Christ to the whole world and beyond. Through the apostles, on whom the Spirit descended, we are drawn into the guidance of the Holy Spirit into all truth, into Christ *the* truth.

[1] The other reason we call the Church apostolic is that it is sent into the world. The Greek *apostello* means "send." The apostles are the ones who are sent into the world, and so is the apostolic Church.

The Formation of Doctrine

Continuing our exploration of how the Spirit guides us into all truth, let's look at the early history of the Church, with a view to how theological teachings came to be expressed. To Christian eyes, these critical centuries vividly reveal the work of the Holy Spirit within the particular events of history.

The idea of the Holy Spirit leading the Church to the truth can sound like we are being led magically by an unseen being. The Holy Spirit does guide us, in time, through human beings, in history, and we ought not overly romanticize the process. When we look at the writings and events of church history, we may at times wonder how anyone could discern the Holy Spirit at work. The processes that led to the Church's great councils, and in many cases the proceedings of the councils themselves and their aftermath, were often politicized and messy. One of the greatest Fathers of the Church, St Gregory the Theologian, presided over portions of the Second Ecumenical Council (A.D. 381), a landmark triumph for the Church and her theology. But he left the event in disgust and went off to write theological poems—many of them laments about church politics and backbiting bishops.

While guarding against an idealized view of church history, we do emphatically take the position that God guides us, that he works with the sinful members of the Church, and that the Church itself is a holy body. Quite clearly this is an interpretation of faith. When we recite the Nicene Creed, we say, "I *believe* in one, holy, catholic, and apostolic Church," making it an article of faith professed alongside our faith in "one God, the Father," "one Lord, Jesus Christ," and "the Holy Spirit." In placing our faith in the Church, we are trusting that in and through all of the complexity of history, in and through the sinners that all of us human beings are, God is at work, making the Church what it is: one, holy, catholic, and apostolic.

This perspective is not universal. Many people, when they learn of sin within the Church and during its formation, conclude that it's impossible that this could be God's holy Church. They lose faith in the entire project or try to dissociate from the early church and attempt to start again, as was the case of the nineteenth-century Restoration Movement within Protestantism. There are also popular books such as Dan Brown's *The Da Vinci Code*, and more academic books such as Elaine Pagels' *The Gnostic Gospels*, that assert that the selection of canonical and authoritative texts was an untrustworthy, male-dominated process that squelched alternative theologies such as those of the Gnostics. But if we take it on faith that the Holy Spirit acts within the Church throughout history, while we may continue to find noncanonical texts attractive or interesting, we also will trust that the theologies that were squelched were not, as a whole, true. But it's not only a matter of trust. To the eye of faith, it's quite plain that the rejected texts did not genuinely bear the gospel of Christ. That gospel is rooted in Christ's passion and his voluntary death on the cross, something conspicuously absent from noncanonical texts.

The process of determining which texts and doctrines are true has been one of elimination; at points it has been a complex and politicized process. But again, faith lets us see that this is how God works, through us sinners and in history. He leads us not by magic, not by compelling people, and not by writing words in the sky, but in and through imperfect people living in imperfect times. There is a genuine engagement between God and people, and also among people.

Theology as Dialogue

Another way of putting it is that the Spirit leads us to true theology through dialogue. Much theological writing takes the form of an exchange between two people or parties. Many theologically formative texts are written in the form of letters, whether they are the epistles of St Paul, St Ignatius, or St Basil the Great, among others. These letters are often declamatory, but they tend to be responses to particular persons or communities with their particular questions and needs, and therefore constitute one side of a dialogue.

Then there is the dialogue of persuasion. The early Christians had to be apologists; in other words, they had to explain themselves to an establishment which had some serious misconceptions about them. Some of the most interesting and formative texts of the early centuries A.D. are dialogues between Christians and persons of other, established faiths; for example, St Justin Martyr's dialogue with Trypho the Jew, or Trajan's correspondence with Pliny, or St Theophilus of Antioch's letter to the pagan Autolychus.

Another use of dialogue—as a manner of exposition—has a long tradition, a high point of which is the imagined dialogues in which Plato set out his thought. Here the genre is a pedagogical method in which the reader observes ideas unfolding and ideally becomes caught up in their internal logic. Christian writers used this method too. St Gregory of Nyssa, for example, set out his thinking in *On the Soul and Resurrection* in the form of a dialogue with his dying sister Macrina (perhaps echoing Plato, who gave Socrates a dialogue with the dying Diotima in *The Symposium*).

But the whole of the development of theology can be described as a dialogue: when we look at the majority of theological breakthroughs in the early centuries of the Church, we are struck by the observation that most of them were written in response to opposing views. Someone teaches that Jesus Christ actually wasn't fully human (for how could God become *human?*), that he wasn't really made of human flesh but instead was something like a phantom. That teaching elicits a response. Late in the first century, St John the Theologian writes, "By this you know the Spirit of God: every spirit which confesses that Jesus Christ has come in the flesh is of God" (1 Jn 4.2). And so we may say that the heresy of Docetism elicited a theology of Christ's true humanity. The heresy of Nestorianism, which taught that the man Jesus Christ and the divine Son of God were effectively two different persons, was the catalyst for the Church's teaching of the divine-humanity of the single person Jesus Christ. Even the heresy of iconoclasm, which forbade the making or the veneration of images, educed for the Church a theology of the icon, as well as a theology of matter.

This is how we human beings come to much of our knowledge: through the process of elimination, or negation. We often begin our journey of understanding and defining something by stating what it isn't. If we're looking for a way to get from New York City to Philadelphia, we might begin by eliminating some options: "Don't take Route 87; avoid the Lincoln Tunnel." Of course, one can't leave it there, but the negative statements act as preliminaries that let us arrive at the positive ones. "Take the George Washington Bridge." "But not during rush hour." (You see how negative and positive statements must balance each other.)

And so, particularly when we are seeking to describe the indescribable, we begin by saying what is not the case about, for example, Jesus. He is not a spirit. He didn't merely pretend to suffer and die. He is not merely a good man. He is not two persons, one divine and one human. These negations must then lead to affirmations. Jesus is fully divine (therefore spiritual, immaterial, timeless) and also fully human (therefore having a human body and soul), and he is one person. It remains our task to explain how both of these can be true at the same time. But there, too, we see the church wrestling with incorrect solutions before it arrives at those we believe are true.

The result is that many of the writings of the Fathers are called "polemical," in that they are written against points of view that are deemed wrong or heretical. *Heresy* comes from a Greek word meaning "choice," but the word in Greek and in translation comes early on in church history to mean a *wrong* choice, a choice made in isolation from the Church, a division from catholicity. The epistles of St Paul and St John allude to specific incorrect views that need to be countered, and St Paul recognizes the need for these wrong factions (the Greek says "heresies") in order for the genuine to be identified (1 Cor 11.19). His point is not that truth needs falsehood. Nor is he signaling some sort of Hegelian determinism, where the opposition of a thesis and its antithesis will necessarily lead to a true synthesis. He is merely articulating his experience, one that is borne out in time: to articulate the truth, we often need first to refute falsehood.

The first centuries of the Church saw the flourishing of a wide variety of opinions and ideas that couldn't all be genuinely true and Christian. Thus in the second century, St Irenaeus of Lyons wrote an entire treatise, *Against the Heresies*, that took on numerous persons and teachings. And countless such patristic texts follow in the ensuing decades and centuries: *Against the Arians*, *Against Eunomius*, *Against Apollinarius*, *Against Nestorius*. These are some of the most important texts in our tradition; they teach us about the person of Christ.

To explore more fully how the polemical texts function, we must understand that polemic in the early church didn't usually conform to the ideal of dialogue held in most Western societies today. It is rarely the kind of dialogue in which two parties strive politely to understand each other, affirm the affirmable in each other's positions, say, "Hmm, yes, I hear where you're coming from, but did you consider . . ." and then take matters to the next level. Early church polemic is bluntly against views judged as heretical, as flat-out wrong. The black-and-white logic of these texts helped to hold the Church together in times of crisis. It is also a part and parcel of their didactic function.

We can look back at these dialogues from a variety of perspectives. They can come across as a story of heroes and villains, Fathers and heretics. And in hindsight we can see truth to that interpretation: St Athanasius, and not Arius, was right about the Son of God. St Cyril of Alexandria, not Nestorius, was right about the person of Christ. The heroes-versus-villains portrait of history is the one that we sing about in church when we celebrate the Church Fathers and the ecumenical councils.

With centuries on centuries of temporal remove from these polemics, however, and with an increasing number of research tools at our fingertips, twentieth- and twenty-first-century scholars have in many cases discovered that the opponents, or heretics, didn't actually teach the degree of heresy that was attributed them by their Orthodox counterparts, who sometimes exaggerated for pedagogical reasons. Perhaps the opponents didn't themselves realize the full extent or the ultimate logical conclusion of what they were teaching. Or perhaps the heresy being condemned was a distortion created by the heretics' hawkish disciples or zealous scribes. It's important for those of us who carefully study history to distinguish between the heresy and its alleged perpetrator.

So it's possible, for example, that Nestorius was not a Nestorian. Or perhaps he was not quite as stupid and impious as St Cyril sometimes said he was. With an honest look back, we can see that sometimes what the Fathers (and we) condemn is something of a construct, an exaggeration; the villains may not be as obviously villainous as described. Does this mean we find ourselves in a sea of demythologized relativism about the formation of doctrine? No. It remains vital to continue to affirm that the heresy of Nestorianism, which was indeed taught by some and continues to appear in various guises today, is wrong and is incompatible with Orthodox Christianity. Nestorianism has therefore served its purpose: it is a relief against which we may all the clearer understand the right teaching about Jesus Christ, begotten of God eternally, the same born of Mary in history. This too is the case for heretical Origenism, whether or not Origen himself subscribed to it in full.

Thus it is that the history of ideas, and the history of the formation of doctrine, is a history of dialogue, of interaction. This is one way the Holy Spirit works within people in particular places and particular times, in the nitty-gritty of history, to elicit what we identify as right-praising, right-teaching Christian theology.

Discernment and Authority

This preliminary investigation leaves us with some important questions. If it's all a matter of give and take between various right and wrong positions over history, how do we know which ones are true and which are false? Who makes that decision, and on what authority? Who was to say, and on what basis, that St Cyril's teaching was right and Nestorianism was wrong?

In answering such questions, we frequently speak about the Church as if it were a person. "The Church teaches that Jesus Christ is both fully divine and fully human." All right, that's fairly straightforward. But then you may hear someone say something more controversial, or perhaps not as clearly established in tradition. "The Church teaches that any form of contraception is a sin." Or, "The Church has never approved of violence in any form." Or you'll read on a website, "The Church teaches that when we die, we pass through aerial tollhouses manned by demons." And you start to wonder, Is this really the Church speaking? Are all of these matters beyond debate? And exactly who is this Church? As one of my colleagues likes to say, "Can you give me an address and a fax number for the church that has made these declarations?"

When we speak in the name of the Church, we're not far from that dangerous place I alluded to earlier in this chapter, where people are liable to claim that their opinions are of the Holy Spirit. We are on a treacherous path when we say too easily that the Church or the Holy Spirit agrees with us, for we just might be making them in our own image.

And yet, there are definitely occasions when we may say, with all proper humility and right piety, as the apostles did in Jerusalem,

"It seemed good to the Holy Spirit and to us" (Acts 15.28) to reason in some way or to embark on some course. We do have criteria to help us discern whether a teaching genuinely is of the Church.

Before I go into those criteria, we need to keep two things in mind about the Church:

1. The Church is the body of Christ (Rom 12.5; 1 Cor 12.12, 27; Eph 4.12; 5.23). This means both that Christ is the head of the Church and that the Church is somehow continuous with the person of Christ and his mission.

2. The Church is composed of particular members, human beings who have been baptized into it. The Church is therefore a council of persons, wherever they exist or existed, and whenever they live or have lived.

There's a certain paradox to these two dimensions of the Church. The Church, as Christ's body and bride, is inherently holy and pure; it is sinless (Eph 5.25–27). Yet it is composed of people like us, all of whom are sinners. We fall short of holiness. We make mistakes, we sin, and, what's more, we are liable also to do so corporately and in the name of the Church itself. But despite having sinners as its members, the Church is sinless. How can we make sense of this paradox?

The two registers of which we speak are not separate entities, as some Reformation theologies suggest—a heavenly, invisible, sinless Church, and an earthly, visible, sinful Church. They are one reality that must be held together. The Church consists of imperfect members, but the Church is more than the sum of its membership. The Church is us, but more than that, the Church is the body that heals us. The Church is the holy hospital, where we come to recall God's image in us. All of this has a bearing on the question of how the Holy Spirit guides us, and how we may discern when it's the Holy Spirit, and not just a band of sinners, speaking in the Church.

How do we know when the Church is speaking? One factor we've discussed is conciliarity: I cannot reason or speak in isolation and be sure that I speak in the name of the Holy Spirit. I rely on conciliarity with others. But that can't be the only safeguard, because I can easily find a group of people who reason as I do; we can start a website and a blog and we're off, beginning what could be our own corporate delusion. So how do we know when the Church is speaking?

Conciliarity with the Church

At the end of the previous chapter, I pointed out the importance of being in council with the Church when we seek to articulate theological truth. We are now ready to ask the question, How do we know when a given teaching is in council with the Church?

To begin with, we have to say that, strictly speaking, we can't know, here and now. We can only make affirmations and back them up, trusting that future generations will discern whether God's Church was speaking. In making such affirmations, it's our responsibility to

    1. explain our criteria and the authority which we give them,

2. show how the teaching in question agrees with our criteria,

3. show how and why the affirmation can reasonably be seen as true.

First, let's consider 1 and 2 together.

To discern whether a teaching is of the Church, our primary criterion is Scripture, the preeminent written expression of God's word. However, we read Scripture "in the Church," which means we read it in light of the Church's tradition. We look to the Church Fathers, and perhaps especially to the distillations of the patristic writing found in the Church's universally received councils and in the Church's hymnography. We look also to other expressions of the Church's life—rituals, feasts, icons, and saints' lives. In the next chapter, I will show more precisely how these sources constitute the Church's tradition. But these are the voices by which the Church speaks: where there's a clear and consistent witness to any given teaching within these sources, that teaching may properly be said to emanate from the Church or be in council with the Church.

One person's expression of the need for the conciliarity of the Church and conciliarity with the Church went as follows. St Vincent of Lérins said in the fifth century that we must "hold to what has been believed everywhere, always and by all." Now, what exactly does he mean? Was there anything that was so universally believed, ever, much less always? Of course, his "everywhere, always, and by all" refers not to all humanity and history but to the world *within the Church*. So one thing he means is that we must hold to the things that have been believed everywhere and always by everyone who is of the Church. He is asserting that, while there may be questions that admit different opinions within the Church (for example, not everyone within the Church believes exactly the same thing about angels), there are teachings that everyone who is of the Church has always believed. These are the key teachings that affect our salvation.

So when we look within the world of Holy Tradition—by reading the Fathers of any century, by praying the liturgy, by studying the ecumenical councils, and by seeing how all of this draws from Holy Scripture—we will find unambiguous answers to some questions, as well as many questions whose answers are still being debated. Some examples of contestable issues: Was the way in which Mary gave birth to Christ virginal, or only the way in which she conceived him? Are we judged once, at the end of the age, or also at the moment of our deaths? How do we reckon the date for the celebration of the Lord's resurrection? To this day we may, and do, argue from Holy Tradition for one or another answer to these questions.

Some of the critical issues for which we do have clarity are: Did God have to create the world, or did he create of his own free will? Is Jesus Christ divine, as God the Father is, or is he a lesser being? Is he really human, as we are, or did he only appear to be so? These questions have unequivocal answers in the Church. They may be expressed variously, but the meaning is both clear and universal. These are among the Church's dogmas. And although they were formulated at specific times and in specific languages, we understand their truth to be universal.

So St Vincent's assertion that we must hold to "what has been believed everywhere, always and by all" refers to those teachings that, since apostolic times, are either explicit or implicit in the entirety of Orthodox Christian tradition. Indeed, if we take the implications of the "Vincentian canon" one step further, we could say that, since God's final revelation in the person of his Son, Jesus Christ, who was crucified and rose for us and for our salvation according to the Scriptures, there are effectively no new teachings. There are, rather, new formulations, new expressions, and new implications drawn from the revelation given us in the person of Jesus Christ as witnessed in Holy Scripture.

No new teachings, but new expressions. Let's look at how this distinction functions throughout history. Over the centuries since the writing of the Scriptures, new questions naturally arose over time, questions that hadn't occurred to previous generations. To give an early example, people in the first century were not vexed by the question of whether Christ had a human soul. But at the end of the fourth century, Christ's human soul became a matter of urgent controversy, threatening to divide the Church. So St Gregory the Theologian and others had to express the teaching that Christ was fully and completely human, of the same composition as us, "body and soul." As St Gregory showed, this was not a new teaching but the formulation of a truth already revealed in the Scriptures. He was careful to prove that his teaching was not in disagreement with anything that authoritative texts had proclaimed before his day. Although Gregory did seem to say something new, he was only giving expression to something that had been believed everywhere, always, and by all who were of the Church.

Today, too, questions arise that were not relevant to the ancients. Many of these new questions come from the bioethical sphere. We have questions about stem-cell research and cloning that couldn't have occurred to the early Church Fathers. There are also more perennial theological questions that aren't inspired by new technologies but simply seem more relevant to us today than they once did, such as questions about gender, and how gender bears on ministry and on love and marriage. There are no early church treatises about why the priesthood is open to males only: the issue was never seriously raised until the twentieth century. There are no conciliar or liturgical tracts on whether it's important that Christ was male, because that question didn't exercise people until recently. But these issues are definitely relevant today. When we Orthodox reflect on these and other new moral or theological issues, we must strive to reason freshly, creatively, and yet in unison (in council) with the voices everywhere and always that together constitute the mind of the Church.[2]

Conciliarity and Authority

The next question is, *Who decides* what is truly in unison with the Church? In a sense, *you* do. Each one of us as a responsible Orthodox Christian should be able to give account for how and why we give authority to the particular elements of our tradition, and how a teaching agrees with those elements. Yet at the same time, as Orthodox Christians, we recognize particular lines of doctrinal authority and responsibility within the Church.

---

[2]There is a good deal of vibrant reflection at the hands of Orthodox theologians and ethicists on the issues mentioned here, and some of their works are listed at the end of this book. Yet one can't help but feel that it's only a beginning; so much remains to be done to provide answers that are both pastorally responsible and genuinely faithful to the Church's tradition.

Bishops, to give an important example, are vested with an authority resting in several dimensions. They preside over the Eucharist. They discern and apply the Church's canons in the particular situations placed before them. But a key part of the episcopal vocation is the discernment and communication of truth, of right theology; bishops are by definition teachers and keepers of the apostolic faith. St Irenaeus writes, "By 'knowledge of the truth' we mean the teaching of the Apostles; the order of the Church as established from earliest times throughout the world, the distinctive stamp of the body of Christ, preserved through the episcopal succession: for to the bishops the Apostles committed the care of the church which is in each place."[3] This is a high calling.

But the bishop's authority is properly exercised in council, not only with other bishops but with the whole Church. In the Orthodox Church there is no eucharistic celebration by a bishop alone without a congregation. The teaching of the Church is not dictated infallibly by any single person, bishop or otherwise. Every person of the Church is responsible to both listen to the bishop and challenge him, should his teaching run counter to the apostolic faith he is charged to discern and to preach. Theological creativity today is exercised throughout the Church; it is the product not only of bishop-teachers but also priests and lay theologians, an age-old Orthodox tradition. At any rate, the bishop's responsibility is to oversee the Church as a council.

And so we return to the theme of conciliarity, a key to the "mechanics of doctrine" that we are exploring in this chapter, one on which rests the authority of the Church. As we continue to ponder the principle of conciliarity, we may observe that it takes

[3]Irenaeus, *Against the Heresies* III.24.i.

a strong degree of humility to exercise it properly. It requires real listening and sacrifice; it requires being open to possibilities other than those we might individually devise or desire.

It also requires time, and often a good deal of it. The theological definitions of the ecumenical councils have incalculable authority in the Church, not just by virtue of their ecumenical composition but also because of their ecumenical reception, their acceptance by the Church. This is where the time-factor figures in. In A.D. 325 the emperor Constantine convened a council to deal with the controversial teachings of Arius that the Son of God was created by God and is therefore a being of a lesser order than God. That council produced the formulation that the Son is "Light from Light, True God from True God, of the same essence as the Father," which was supposed to put the issue to rest. But as history tells it, the issue was not settled for many decades. No episcopal authority could solve it. The Arian position gained ascendancy for a considerable period; in the middle of the fourth century, the majority of Christians in the empire were Arians. So if right now we were to find ourselves in mid-fourth-century Asia Minor, we might have a very difficult time knowing which position was the orthodox one: that of Arius or that of Athanasius, who was exiled three times by the Arian emperor for his position. But with the passage of several decades, Arius' position was rejected, the Arian councils were disowned, and the Nicene council convened in 325 became universally accepted—an ecumenical council, the first council to have that status.

We have thus come to another important fact about the mechanics of doctrine and of Church authority. In some cases it's only hindsight that shows us who was orthodox and who heretical. It's a matter of time, waiting to see which position is ultimately received as the position of the Church. But hindsight is critical. We may look back at any point in the history of the Church and see the positions that were vindicated and those that were rejected. And it's on the basis of those vindications and rejections that we must discern the continued debates on theological, moral, and ethical matters to this day.

We have now briefly sketched the criteria for assessing whether a teaching is genuinely "of the Church." But even if we have mastered these, it is still incumbent upon us to *explain* the Church's teachings, to show why we hold them to be true. Moreover, if any teaching is to be considered a dogmatic or binding teaching of the Church, we have to explain how and why it is truly a matter of our salvation. I will say more on this in the last chapter. But for now let's recall that we don't believe dogmas because they are dogmas; we believe them because we hold them to be true. And a key part of discerning the teachings of the Church is explaining them to ourselves and to each other, understanding their truth. We don't do this merely to cater to modern rationalism. The Church's mission to the whole world is to preach and explain to our hearers what we believe to be the truth. It's a matter of taking the Church's teachings to heart and engaging them in the whole of our being. This is what it means to be a faithful Christian, and a whole person.

chapter six

"HOW DO YOU READ?" GLEANING THEOLOGY FROM THE TRADITION

> *I have written in accordance with what I have understood both from contemplation on the Scriptures, and also from those who speak the truth, and a little from experience itself.*

> —St Isaac the Syrian, Homily 14

These unassuming words of St Isaac the Syrian, taken from one of his ascetical homilies, are indicative of how people of the Church have gone about discerning theology. Note three basic points. The Holy Scriptures are mentioned foremost as the ground of theological reflection. One who seeks to reason theologically must be grounded, as St Isaac puts it, in contemplation on the Scriptures.

Second, we do not stop at the Bible. We must listen to "those who speak the truth" (or, as another translation of the text has it, from "true mouths"); the Bible is an intricate and diverse collection of texts, requiring a right interpretation. As the eunuch said to the apostle Philip, "How can I understand the Scriptures, unless someone guides me?" (Acts 8.31).

Third, St Isaac acknowledges that our theological reflection also relies on our experience of life. Our perceptions and thoughts may delude us, and therefore they need to be checked. But we do not ignore our experience, our perception, and our mind. We bring them to the service of our understanding; theology should ring true to our experience.

But note as well that St Isaac then says, "I have taken no little trouble to write these things," reminding us that none of this is simple or easy for anyone. Finding and articulating theology, the truth about God, challenges us to the very limits of our mental, spiritual, and even physical capacities. Nonetheless, we affirm together with St Isaac and the Fathers that it's not only a possible task but the worthiest of all tasks. So let's explore the kinds of data which people of the Church draw on to discern theology. We have been given a wealth of material, but what matters is what we do with it. How do we read it and how do we make sense of it?[1]

We've identified Scripture as our prime source. Scripture is read through the patristic legacy, the Church's liturgical life, the ecumenical councils, the saints, and even the Church's iconography and architecture. These are the particular expressions of God's revelation that constitute our theological sources (or, if we may borrow the medieval Western term, *loci theologici*, "places of theology"). Let's examine these broadly, while keeping in mind the following questions:

---

[1]The title of this chapter is a quotation from Lk 10.26.

* To which texts, rites, or symbols are we referring?

* How are they read and understood in the Church?

* What is the nature and extent of their authority in the Church?

* How do they relate to each other in the broader tradition of the Church?

* Are there factors we should bear in mind to inform our reading and understanding?

Scripture

> *It is impossible either to say or fully to understand anything about God beyond what has been divinely proclaimed to us by the sacred declarations of the Old and New Testaments.*
>
> —St John of Damascus,
> *Exact Exposition of the Orthodox Faith*

> *How can I understand unless someone guides me?*
>
> —Acts 8.31

As mentioned earlier, the Bible is not simply one among a list of sources from which we come to know about God and the world. It is the authoritative written witness of God's self-revelation. There is no truth in the Church that is not scriptural truth: nothing that isn't based on what is given us in the Bible. All of the other expressions of the Church's tradition—patristic, liturgical, conciliar, and canonical—must be shown to be biblical, even as their very function is to read and interpret the Bible rightly.

Scripture and Tradition

The history of Western Christianity has seen a particular debate about the authority of Scripture. The Reformation emphasis on the authority of Scripture alone (*sola scriptura*) was countered in the Roman Catholic Church with the teaching that authority rests in Scripture and Tradition. Tradition, in this understanding, means the various authoritative texts and rites apart from Scripture, and thus constitutes a parallel source alongside Scripture, which is why it is referred to as the "two-source theory." It remains common, particularly in the Christian West, to conceive of Tradition along these lines.

By specifying "Scripture *and* Tradition," the two-source idea rightly retains the special place of Scripture among the authoritative sources. The problem is that Tradition isn't just a compendium of texts; it's a way of reading Scripture. The word Tradition, it must be said, is used to cover many (too many) ideas, and I would propose the following attempt at summarizing the main ways we may conceive of Tradition.

Tradition is an *activity* or *dynamism*; it is the "handing down" or "handing over" of faith and practice from one person to another, one generation to another. It is an ongoing activity, which is why we continue to speak of "the living Tradition."

Tradition is *content* only insofar as we point to specific texts and practices that are "part of the tradition." These texts and practices are the instruments of the handing down of the faith; compositely they form the lens through which we read Scripture.

Tradition is, as Vladimir Lossky put it, the unique *mode of receiving the truth* that is found in Scripture. Or as Georges Florovsky put it, it is Scripture rightly understood.

Let's dwell on this last point, first by allowing Lossky to complete his thought. He says, "Tradition is not the content of revelation, but the light that reveals it; it is not the word, but the living breath which makes the word heard at the same time as the silence from which it came; it is not the truth, but a communication of the Spirit of truth, outside which the truth cannot be received. 'No one can say "Jesus is Lord" except by the Holy Spirit' (1 Cor 12.3)."[2]

Tradition is therefore associated closely with the Holy Spirit, who inspires not just the writing but the reading of Scripture. In a sense, the reading of Scripture "in the tradition" begins with the writing of the New Testament, where we come to see the Scriptures (meaning the Old Testament) interpreted entirely in the light of Jesus Christ. Subsequently, the Old and the New Testaments continue to be read in the tradition, which means both in the Holy Spirit and in the light of the Church's patristic, conciliar, and liturgical witness.

The relationship between Scripture and Tradition is circular. Tradition represents the right reading of Scripture. But how do we identify what is of Tradition? By referring to Scripture. So something is traditional only if it is scriptural, but we rightly read Scripture only in Tradition.

[2]"Tradition and Traditions," in *In the Image and Likeness of God* (Crestwood, NY: St Vladimir's Seminary Press, 1985), 151–52.

Before this sounds too self-contradictory, let's see how it has operated in history. During the composition of the creed at the Council of Nicea, a debate arose over the word *homoousios*. That word, which means "of the same essence," was vital in correcting the prevalent misconception that the Son of God is a lesser being than the Father. No, the Nicene Fathers said, the Son is "of the same essence," the same *being* as the Father; the Son is *homoousios* with the Father. But a concern arose that this word doesn't appear in Scripture and therefore should not form a part of the creed. What settled the debate is vitally important to the history of theology. The meaning of the word was shown to be *scriptural,* with reference to Jesus' scriptural statements of his oneness with the Father. And so the word was accepted as properly belonging in the creed, a benchmark of the tradition that interprets Scripture. We have therefore identified not a circle but a spiral, Tradition and Scripture working with each other in a particular relationship to convey, or "to tradition," the gospel.

The Contents of Scripture

In the understanding of the New Testament authors, and for a considerable period of time afterward, "the Scriptures" generally referred to what we call the Old Testament. Jesus frequently berates his inquirers for not knowing the Scriptures; moreover he (together with the evangelists and St Paul) again and again shows how the Scriptures refer to him and are fulfilled in him. What we call the New Testament, then, is technically not more Scripture in addition to the Old Testament but the fulfillment of the Scriptures. Of course, there's the broader usage of the term *the Scriptures* that includes the New Testament. But we do well to remember that the Old Testament is the Scriptures that are fulfilled by the New

Testament. And we shall see why when we discuss further how the Scriptures are read in light of Christ.

The Scriptures, Old and New Testaments, are a vast assembly of texts with a variety of forms and functions. And yet their assemblage was anything but a random or arbitrary process. Considering the books we call canonical Scripture, we do well to remember two realities. One is the fact of a clear body of Scripture whose books are judged as canonical or truth-bearing; the other is a certain flexibility to the content of that body of texts.

Canon means "measure" or "standard": the canonical Scriptures are those which are understood as "measuring up," books which conform to and lead us to the gospel, the apostolic understanding of Christ. So the "canon of Scripture" is very much a reality, even if we're not finally talking about a single fixed and dogmatized list of books but rather a measure or criterion according to which the scriptural books are judged to be authoritative.

This all begins to make more sense when we consider the historical process by which the books of canonical Scripture were recognized. Many accounts of Jesus' life were written in the late first and early second centuries. Relatively early on, certain books were identified as canonical and others as clearly noncanonical. That process took familiar contours: just as the development of doctrine was in large part the refutation of heresies, the canon of Scripture was likewise in great part a process of elimination. In the Church's early encounters with other systems and religions, Gnostic and otherwise, many texts were identified as leading people away from the gospel message; they were therefore excluded, as noncanonical.

While the rejection of these books by the Church is clear and final, the list of accepted books was never quite as simply fixed. The New Testament, in the twenty-seven books we identify today in our Bibles, was codified by the mid-fourth century, if not earlier.[3] Yet this number was not binding for a long time; Revelation, Second Peter, and Second and Third John were not universally accepted for centuries.

Other, we could say more final, settlements of biblical canonicity took place considerably later, in the seventh century. But even now, while we would say that the New Testament's twenty-seven books form a closed and fixed list, we have also a wider list that would include what are sometimes called the "deuterocanonical" (meaning "secondarily canonical") or "apocryphal" books, writings that are not in the Hebrew Bible but do appear in the Septuagint.[4] These books are used in the Church's liturgical life, are referred to by the Fathers, and are certainly regarded as Scripture in the Orthodox Church.

In conclusion, when we refer to the Scriptures in the Orthodox Church, we refer to the wider list: the thirty-nine Old Testament books and the twenty-seven New Testament books we would find

---

[3]St Athanasius lists the books in his Paschal homily of A.D. 367, but we find proximities to this list in the texts of Irenaeus and Tertullian.

[4]The Septuagint (often abbreviated LXX) is the Greek translation of the Hebrew Bible, dating from the second century B.C. It is the version of Old Testament Scripture which the Greek fathers used exclusively. The so-called deuterocanonical texts that are received in Orthodox tradition are First and Second Esdras, Tobit, Judith, Additions to Esther, Wisdom of Solomon, Ecclesiasticus, Baruch, Letter of Jeremiah, Daniel and Susanna, Bel and the Dragon, the Prayer of Manasseh, First through Fourth Maccabees, the Prayer of Azariah, and the Song of the Three Youths.

in a typical Protestant Bible, together with the additional writings found in the Septuagint.[5] The Church Fathers, the Church's liturgy, and the Church's iconography all draw on these texts as the written word of God.

How the Church Reads the Scriptures

As I've noted, Scripture is not self-interpreting. We see well how over history the same Scriptures have been made to support a broad variety of views. Orthodox and heretics alike used and cited the same Bible. And so do all of today's Christian denominations, which number in the thousands, many of whose teachings are at considerable odds with each other.[6] Jews come to some quite different conclusions reading the same Law, Prophets, and Psalms as Christians do; so do Muslims. As St Irenaeus of Lyons famously said, the Scriptures are like the tiles of a mosaic that

---

[5]The contents of canonical Scripture are spelled out helpfully in Petros Vassiliadis, "Canon and Authority of Scripture: An Orthodox Hermeneutical Perspective," in S. T. Kimbrough, ed., *Orthodox and Wesleyan Scriptural Understanding and Practice* (Crestwood, NY: St Vladimir's Seminary Press, 2005), 21–35. The books Orthodox accept as canonical can be found together in one book in English translation in the *Oxford Annotated Bible*. The Revised Standard Version is preferable to the New Revised Standard Version, which, in its intention to reduce unnecessarily gender-specific language, has in many cases compromised the intended meaning of the text. I should also mention that while the narrower list of canonical Scripture is essentially shared among Christians, the books included in a wider canon may vary, especially among the non-Chalcedonian churches.

[6]Whether they acknowledge it or not, virtually every Christian church or group has a tradition through which they read Scripture. Most Reformation Christians may profess the authority of "Scripture alone" but will at the same time give a markedly privileged authority to the Reformers' reading of Scripture and to the subsequent interpretive tradition which evolved after them.

---

rightly compose a picture of a king (Christ) but that can just as easily be rearranged to make a picture of a dog or a fox.[7]

Our question then is, How do we get the mosaic of the King?

The Church's primary answer is, Start with the King.

Scripture Is about Jesus Christ

We understand the Bible to be God's divinely inspired word, expressed humanly. This sounds similar to how we describe Jesus Christ: God's Word, humanly expressed. In some ways, therefore, the Scriptures share with Jesus Christ a divine-and-human, or "theanthropic," character. They are timeless, yet very much marked by the time that produced them. But the connection between the Bible and Christ doesn't stop there. The exegesis (the reading and understanding) of Scripture is the exegesis of Christ. Christ is the hermeneutical or interpretive key of Scripture.

The writing of the Old Testament chronologically preceded the historical coming of Jesus Chris; they were not written in the conscious, explicit knowledge of Jesus of Nazareth. As far as the human authors and the Jewish audience were concerned, they were written about the people of Israel and God's relationship with his chosen people. The "Suffering Servant" of Isaiah didn't signify "the Messiah" to all Jews; messiahship in general was understood by many in more political than personal terms. The author of Exodus did not have the cross of Christ in his mind when writing about Moses' staff; neither did the Jewish readers of Exodus.

---

[7]*Against the Heresies* 1.8.1.

But Christ and the cross changed how the Scriptures were read. We now see that Isaiah was writing about Jesus' birth, that Jesus is the Suffering Servant, the Messiah. The Gospels record Jesus' talking of the Scriptures this way: he says that Moses, the traditional author of the Pentateuch, was writing about *him* (Jn 5.46). In St Luke's gospel, Jesus begins his earthly ministry by showing how Isaiah 61 applies to himself (Lk 4.18–21). But it's only after the cross that this understanding of the Scriptures is truly opened to the disciples. On the road to Emmaus, the risen Lord walks with the disciples: "And beginning with Moses and all the prophets, he interpreted to them in all the Scriptures the things concerning himself" (Lk 24.27). The Law, the Prophets, and even the Psalms were all written about him (Lk 24.44). It's almost impossible to overstate this vital point: Christ and the cross changed everything about how the Scriptures were read.

From the Christian perspective, then, the Old Testament Scriptures were written to reveal Jesus Christ. When St Paul writes, "We have this treasure in earthen vessels" (2 Cor 4.7), he is saying that the treasure is something that needs to be found, unearthed from the vessels. As he puts it earlier in the same passage, the gospel is veiled, and it must be revealed; the veil must be lifted. As we see from the closing of St Luke's gospel, Christ lifts the veil. Or to put it another way, it is the Spirit who lifts the veil to reveal Christ. That, at any rate, is how St Paul expresses it. He writes of the Jews that "to this day, when they read the old covenant, that same veil remains unlifted, because only through Christ is it taken away. Yes, to this day whenever Moses is read a veil lies over their minds; but when a man turns to the Lord the veil is removed. Now the Lord is the Spirit, and where the Spirit of the Lord is, there is freedom" (2 Cor 3.14–17).

The risen Lord opens the Scriptures to his disciples, and from that point on, they, and through them the Fathers and the whole tradition of the Church, read the Scriptures anew. We read them by the Holy Spirit in the light of Christ. And so we have it once again: the Spirit guides us into all truth precisely by guiding us to Christ.

A Variety of Ways of Reading

Bearing in mind this basic and vital point about the Christ-centered reading of Scripture, we ought to note that the Church interprets Scripture in a variety of different ways, all of which conspire to depict Christ. We have noted that the Scriptures encompass a great variety of genres: creation stories, parables, genealogies, histories, prayers, apocalyptic passages, prophecies, poetry, wisdom literature, and letters. Any single scriptural book may contain more than one of these types of literature; we do well to be conscious of them and read accordingly. Our exploration in chapter 3 of parts of the book of Genesis is an example of a reading that is attentive to the intended function of a text and to the Church's use of it.

Owing in part to this variety of genres in the Bible, the Church does not read it as one long string of undifferentiated data. Different texts have different functions and significance; a single text can also be read in various ways to glean from it different points. St Ephrem of Syria writes,

> If there only existed a single sense for the words of scripture, then the first commentator who came along would discover it, and other hearers would experience neither the labor of searching, nor the joy of finding. Rather, each word of our Lord has its own form, and each form has its

own members, and each member has its own character. Each individual understands according to his capacity and interprets as it is granted to him.[8]

Even the New Testament authors approach Old Testament Scriptures in a variety of ways, both literal and spiritual. In his Letter to the Galatians, St Paul interprets Abraham and his seed in highly metaphorical terms: Abraham's offspring is taken to mean not his immediate offspring but Christ (3.16). Abraham's two wives are symbols of (St Paul calls them "allegories") the two covenants, the old and the new Jerusalem (Gal 4.24–31). In Romans 10.18, St Paul takes a passage from the Psalms that speaks of the planets and stars (19.4) and applies it to the missionaries: "Their voice has gone out to all the earth, and their words to the ends of the world." To this day, we use a verse about astronomy to sing of the apostles in the Church.

Thus, Moses' ascent on Mount Sinai is understood both as the way he came to encounter the Lord and receive the commandments, as well as (at the hands of St Gregory of Nyssa and others) an allegory for every human being's spiritual ascent to the cloud of "dazzling darkness" where we meet God. The "little ones," Babylonian children who are "dashed against the rock" in Psalm 137.9, are not the imagined subjects of a brutal Israelite vengeance on their oppressors; they are interpreted as the passions, which must be killed when they are still "little."

There is a great deal of differentiation applied to the Church's reading of the Scriptures; it's anything but a fundamentalist reading. The first line of demarcation, as we've seen, is between the

[8]*Commentary on the Diatessaron* 7.22.

Old Testament (Scripture) and the New Testament (its fulfill-ment). This basic distinction allows for one of the most fruitful and classical modes of Christian understanding of the Old Testa-ment: reading the figures and stories in the Old Testament as types that are fulfilled in the New Testament. This is known as typol-ogy. From the New Testament onward, elements of the Scriptures are read as types that are waiting to be fulfilled in Jesus Christ and in the persons and events that surround him. A reading of the Let-ter to the Hebrews alone would be enough of an illustration. In Hebrews, the Old Testament priesthood and multiple sacrificial offerings for the errors of the people are but shadows that are illu-mined and fulfilled in Christ, the High Priest, with his once-for-all blood sacrifice of himself for the errors of the people.

Both the New Testament and subsequent writing and liturgical hymnography interpret Old Testament events and persons typo-logically: Moses' staff is a type of the cross (as are the trees in Par-adise); the Jewish Passover is a type of Christ's passion; the temple (especially the Holy of Holies) is a type of Mary. The examples are countless, and they are foundational to our understanding of the nature and function of Scripture, particularly its function of revealing Christ.

What can be called a "critical reading" of Scripture is also a con-sistent feature of the Church's interpretation, if by critical we mean analytical and not disapproving. Since the early centuries there has been an awareness of the necessity of discerning both literal and spiritual truth in Scripture, and more generally of the need to bring contemporary scientific and linguistic knowledge to bear on one's reading. Hence St Basil the Great, in his *Homilies on the Hexae-meron*, is found to be applying the cosmology of his own day to his (quite literalist) reading of the first chapter of Genesis. Origen was explicit about the difference between historical material in the Bible and that which is written for its spiritual meaning alone.[9] To assist the scholarly study of the Scriptures, Origen compiled his remarkable *Hexapla*, a side-by-side presentation of Old Testament texts in six Greek and Hebrew versions. As part of our own, contemporary deep engagement with Scripture, we bring to bear on our reading whatever resources we have: the close analysis of words, of literature and literary genre, of the development of texts over history, of the factors of orality and literacy.

Once again, a fundamentalist reading of Scripture is utterly foreign to Orthodoxy, which has always admitted a variety of approaches to the same scriptural texts. Sometimes these approaches were characteristic of entire schools or traditions of thought. Some tended toward an allegorical reading of Scripture, while the others rested with an exegesis based more on historicity and literal interpretation. As methodologies, they may have opposed each other to a certain extent. Yet the Church embraces both, in the service of uncovering all of the potential for truth behind the written word.

Indeed, to adhere as fundamentalists do to the "inerrancy of Scripture" is irrelevant because, as I've suggested throughout this book, the entire point rests with the right (or "inerrant," if you must) *reading* of Scripture. Of course Scripture is utterly unique as God's word, but it was written by human hands. We stand by

---

[9]Book IV of his *On First Principles* is devoted to Origen's understanding of Scripture, its inspiration, and how it is to be read, and chapter 3 is particularly explicit on the matter of spiritual and historical interpretation. As mentioned earlier [chapter 3, note 10], these portions of Origen's work did not figure into the "Origenism" that was later condemned by the Church.

St Paul's classic utterance: "All scripture is inspired by God and profitable for teaching, for reproof, for correction, and for training in righteousness, that the man of God may be complete, equipped for every good work" (2 Tim 3.16–17). But we take that together with 2 Peter 1.20, which says that "no prophecy of scripture is a matter of one's own interpretation." Scripture will not get you anywhere if you read it incorrectly; the inspired writing of Scripture requires an inspired reading or interpretation of Scripture. As St Hilary of Poitiers said, "Scripture is not in the reading, but in the understanding;"[10] the right understanding is gained in the tradition of the Church. That is the very function of Tradition: rightly to understand Scripture.

Liturgy

> *But when I thought how to understand this,*
> *it seemed to me a wearisome task,*
> *until I went into the sanctuary of God;*
> *then I perceived . . .*
> —Psalm 73.16–17

> *We have seen the true light,*
> *We have received the Heavenly Spirit,*
> *We have found the true faith,*
> *Worshipping the undivided Trinity,*
> *For the Trinity has saved us!*
> —From the Divine Liturgy

[10] *Ad Constantium Aug.* II.9, cited in Georges Florovsky, *Bible, Church, Tradition* (Vaduz: Büchervertriebsanstalt, 1987), 75.

When we consider the liturgy as a source of the Church's theology, we have two aspects in mind. One is liturgical *life*, a life of prayer and sacrament. The other is the actual *texts* that are said, chanted, or sung during the church services.

The Liturgical Life of the Church

We saw in St Luke's account of the encounter on the road to Emmaus how Christ opened the disciples' eyes to the understanding of the Old Testament Scriptures. The account continues, telling us that "when he was at table with them, he took the bread and blessed, and broke it, and gave it to them. And their eyes were opened and they recognized him" (Lk 24.30–31). We may say that the opening of the disciples' eyes, the burning of their hearts, the illumination of their understanding, was a process, one that involved both Christ's preaching and his Eucharist.[11] As we continue the Lukan account to its close, we find the natural reaction to this new understanding and the continuation of its process: "And they were continually in the temple, blessing God" (24.53).

A right understanding of the gospel rests on divine revelation through Holy Scripture and its preaching; it culminates in the continued life of liturgical worship and sacramental participation.

Liturgical life is a vital component of the search for true theology. More than that: liturgical life, by which we mean the way of corporate prayer and sacramental participation, is integral to being human. The human person is by nature a being who praises and gives thanks to God, raising up all of creation to God. In more technical language, we can say that the human person is by nature

---

[11]The wording of this scriptural passage deliberately refers to the virtually identical phrasings in the Last Supper accounts of Matthew, Mark, and Luke.

a doxological, eucharistic, priestly being. This means simply that we are never more ourselves than when we are praising and thanking God, offering his world up to him.[12]

Theology and Prayer

About the search for theology, one of the most oft-cited patristic quotations comes from Evagrius of Pontos, who said, "The theologian is one who truly prays; one who truly prays is a theologian."[13] Prayer and theology are interdependent; one leads to the other. Theology has for centuries been the subject of academic study, because it is indeed highly fascinating to trace the history of ideas and their interrelation. But true theology can't result from a cold and detached academic pursuit. We have to rely on God, put our trust in him, and subject our reason to him to conform it to his image.

There are places in the liturgy where we pray specifically for illumination so that we may understand the truth. We keep coming back to the verses from Psalm 119: "Blessed are you, O Lord, teach me your statutes. Blessed are you, O Master, make me to understand your commandments. Blessed are you, O Holy One, enlighten me with your precepts." The following prayer always precedes the reading of the Gospel during the Divine Liturgy (many Orthodox also use it at home before reading Scripture):

[12]Note how Romans 1.21 identifies the darkening and down-turning of people's minds with their refusal to glorify and give thanks to God.

[13]*Chapters on Prayer*, trans. J. E. Bamberger (Spencer, MA: Cistercian, 1970), 65.

Illumine our hearts, O Lord and lover of mankind, with the light of your divine knowledge, and open the eyes of our understanding, so that we may comprehend the message of your Gospel. Instill in us also reverence for your blessed commandments, so that having conquered sinful desires, we may pursue a spiritual life, thinking and doing all things that are pleasing in your sight. For you are the illumination of our souls and bodies, O Christ our God, and unto you we render glory, together with your eternal Father and your all-holy, gracious and life-giving Spirit; now and ever, and unto the ages of ages. Amen.

In the Prayer of the Hours, a regularly repeated prayer in the liturgical cycle, we ask God, "Sanctify our souls. Purify our bodies. Correct our minds. Cleanse our thoughts." During the thanksgiving prayers after receiving Holy Communion, we say, "Cleanse my soul and sanctify my reasonings. . . . Illumine my five senses."

We know that we are subject to both personal and corporate delusion, and so we know that we need to be illumined by God himself. We therefore have to open ourselves to that illumination explicitly and intentionally, ever prepared to be "transformed by the renewal of our minds" (Rom 12.2), which means being prepared to reconceive God, if our conception is false. This openness involves a combination of right living, a conscious struggle to redirect our passions, as well as attentive private and corporate prayer.

Theology and Liturgy

Obviously, liturgy is more than a corporate petition for the illumination of our hearts and minds. It is the assembly of the people of

God, gathered for the praise and worship of God. In this context, and particularly in the context of the eucharistic liturgy, the Church is most clearly manifest for what it is: the body of Christ, the sign of God's kingdom already given to us and accessible to us. We Christians are "not of this world," and although we are in the world and rejoice in its created beauty and glory, we are also foreigners here. The Church and its liturgy are our home. This is not merely an abstract observation; many worshipers experience quite tangibly that when they are in the Church's liturgy, they are where they belong. And through the multiple hours that a typical Orthodox service might last, even if the singing is off or the children too noisy, they feel there's no better place to be.

Furthermore, the liturgical context is what produced our Scriptures, much of which are written codifications of prayers, chronicles, and recitals of God's acts for his people that took shape in and for the context of the assembly of God. The liturgical life of the Church is the evolution of that same assembly and thus forms the proper context for hearing the Scriptures, for preaching and teaching theology. And so it is that the Fathers and Mothers who lived and wrote the theological and ascetical treatises were also people utterly steeped in the Church's liturgy.

Theology and Sacrament

The liturgical dimension of Orthodox Christian life is described by the gathering of the people of God for praise and worship, and for the offering of ourselves and each other and everything else up to God. This is the very nature of the gathering itself, and of the texts we say and sing and the liturgical actions we perform. All of this taken together constitutes a particular ethos of prayer, the foundation that underlies all of the cultural variations in what we see, taste, touch, hear, and smell in the liturgical life. This life, again, is the context for the learning of the truth, since it's the context for the hearing of the only truth that really matters: the saving gospel of God and his Christ.

But the liturgical life of the Church is not only the sights and sounds, the "smells and bells" as they are sometimes called, nor is it just the texts that are sung. It is also the sacramental dimension of the Church.

Put briefly, a sacrament is something that unites God to the things of the world and unites the things of the world to God. If we understand sacraments in this broad sense, we are liberated from the limited and rather arbitrary classification of seven sacraments sometimes adopted from the Roman Catholic and Protestant West. In this broader kind of thinking, the Church itself is a sacrament, joining together the divine and the human, the uncreated and the created, the eternal and the historical. And the sacrament of sacraments is Christ, who in his person unites God and man.

Still, there are particular rites that we specifically identify as sacraments or "mysteries." From the earliest time of the Church's existence these were baptism and the Eucharist, the two rites that encapsulate the life and meaning of the Church. Baptism is the act by which we die to the "old Adam"—to distorted relationship with God and the world—and put on the "New Adam," Christ (Rom 6.5–11). Baptism is the rite of entry into the whole life of the Church, which is life in Christ. Baptism is unrepeatable; the Eucharist, on the other hand, is ongoing as part of the cycle of our lives. Partaking of the Eucharist, we remember Christ's sacrificial passion and death, we offer our own sacrifice (of ourselves and each other, and of the bread and wine that will become our spiritual food), and we partake of Christ's own body. The Eucharist is the context for the consecration of bishops and the other clergy, as well as for the primary exercise of their authority, which is not only a liturgical and church-disciplinary authority but also a teaching authority.

The sacramental life embraces the totality of life in the world: marriage, ordination, monastic tonsure, penance, burial, and the blessing of water and of other staples of life. In each case we invoke God's Spirit to sanctify, bless, and unite us to each other and to God. The sacramental life is the dynamic work of God in history and in matter, in our lives and in the very stuff of the world; it is the core of the Church's life, inherent to the Church's nature and purpose. Those who would seek rightly to understand and articulate the Church's teachings need to be full participants in that life.

The Texts of the Liturgy

The liturgy is the context for theological reflection and articulation. Its texts are also an integral part of the source material from which we discern the Church's doctrine. The daily, weekly, and annual cycles of the Church are marked by services—Matins, Hours, Vespers, Compline, Typika, the Divine Liturgy—with texts that are appointed for each. These texts combine fixed portions with prayers and hymns that vary daily and weekly.

The texts of the liturgy all share certain characteristics.

Dependability

Local churches may adapt the texts to a certain degree, and parishes will not use the full complement of texts and rites (only a few contemporary monasteries apply them in their complete form). Nevertheless, both the fixed and the variable texts are prescribed by the Church; the local adaptations are done in accordance with established norms, in consultation with the bishop.

The set character of our texts is a highly significant factor for Orthodox liturgical life. The fact that Orthodox Christians gathered almost anywhere in the world are singing and doing more or less the same thing (calendar differences notwithstanding) has a profoundly unifying effect on the Church. Perhaps more importantly, however, the fixed character of our liturgical texts means that they are spiritually and theologically dependable.

The texts of the liturgy are for the most part many centuries old. The fact that they have been said and sung by Christians over this time is testimony to their acceptance by the Church. We are not singing anyone's opinion or new idea. We're singing words that have been tried and tested as true. So when we walk into an Orthodox church, we know what we will be singing and doing. But even if we don't know all of the words ahead of time, we trust utterly that these words will not lead us astray, that they are the Church's words.

We vary, of course, in some of the prayers we may add in response to particular events or concerns. Music, vestments, art, and architecture also differ according to the cultural, geographical, and even economic context. More generally, the Church's liturgy evolves over time, even if the extreme hardships undergone by Orthodox churches in recent centuries have necessitated a certain slowing of that evolution. But the overall textual composition of our liturgy is firmly established.

This is important theologically: it means the liturgical texts can be trusted as representing and feeding the Church's theological reflection. An ancient saying of St Prosper of Aquitaine goes *lex orandi lex est credendi,* which means "what we pray is what we believe." This can be the case only when what we pray is affirmed and received by the Church, and when that reception is proven by the endurance of these texts day after day, week after week, year after year.

Right Reading

The theological dependability of liturgical texts, which rests in part in their *de facto* reception over the years, also rests on their being read in the right way. As with Scripture, and with anything we take in through our senses, much depends on how we understand it. As with Scripture, liturgical texts embrace several different genres. Some texts are sheerly theological:

> The only begotten Son shone timelessly from the Father,
> But from you [O Virgin] he was ineffably incarnate:
> God by nature, yet man for our sake,
> Not two persons, but one, known in two natures![14]

Theological texts in the liturgy can be quite dense. They are composed by and for those who are conversant with theological and philosophical jargon. They reflect specific controversies and their respective outcomes.

Whether hymns are teaching theology, elucidating Scripture, exulting in a feast or in its chief characters, they usually convey

---

[14]Dogmatikon for Tone 6, Vespers.

their message by means of the kind of language that has long been known to be especially appropriate to theology: the language of poetry. Here we aren't receiving or producing strings of data. We are singing. And as we sing, we listen, and as we listen to the poetry, we enter into a living relationship with the Word therein.

There are liturgical hymns about God, the Virgin Mary, the saints; there are hymns recounting stories from saints' lives. Most of these hymns are addressed to the persons in question, as hymns of praise. There are hymns that explain feasts, always bringing us into the feast and the feast into our lives. Such hymns often begin by emphasizing the eternal character of the feast, bringing it into the "eternal today": "Yesterday I was crucified with you, today I rise with you," we sing at Pascha. At the Feast of the Nativity we sing:

> Today the Virgin gives birth to the transcendent one,
> And the earth offers a cave to the unapproachable one.
> Angels with shepherds glorify him,
> The wise-men journey with the star.
> For unto us is the eternal God born as a little child.

As with Scripture and with the saints' lives, liturgical hymns may include stories, images, and symbols. At the Feast of the Entrance of the Theotokos into the Temple, we sing that the Virgin Mary enters the Holy of Holies as a little girl and lives there, fed manna by the angels. At the Feast of the Dormition of the Theotokos, we sing that the apostles were carried on clouds from the ends of the earth to be at Mary's funeral. We interpret these in the spirit in which the hymns were composed.[15] They

---

[15]Many of the images and events described in the feast days of Mary are taken from the *Protoevangelion of James*, a text originating in the second century.

convey spiritual truth, the truth about Mary's piety and purity, the truth about the apostles' love for her and about their mystical presence at her deathbed.

Rightly understood within the life of the Church, liturgical texts are words of grace, life, and truth. They are expressions of theology, examples of the Church's reading of Scripture, and criteria for theological discernment. They are a sure means by which the Holy Spirit guides us into all truth.

Scripture in the Liturgy

We have looked at some of the different ways that the Church's tradition reads the Scriptures. That reading takes place not only through the writings of the Fathers and through the definitions and canons of the ecumenical councils, but also through the liturgy. In fact, taking into account how much the Psalter is read and cited in the liturgical services, as well as the readings and citations from the rest of the Bible, we can say that the vast majority of what is heard in Church is taken directly from Scripture. Let's look at some of the ways in which the liturgy works with Scripture.

Through Psalmody and Quotation from the Psalms

A substantial portion of the liturgical life of the Orthodox Church takes the form of the recitation of the psalms. This is especially the case in monastic settings, where the daily offices are dominated by psalmody. (In a traditional monastic setting, the entire Psalter is read in church in the course of any given week.) In monastic settings as well as in parish contexts, the psalms are the blood coursing through the veins of the Church's liturgy.

The Church's hymns, as well as verses interspersed between them and preceding Scripture readings, are often quotations of the psalms. These are quotations whose context dictates the meaning that the Church intends for us to take. When we recite Psalm 116.13, "I will lift up the cup of salvation and call on the name of the Lord," in the context of Holy Communion, we interpret it entirely in terms of its eucharistic implications.

Through the Church's Lectionary

The liturgy works with Scripture also in the way it selects texts for particular services. There are readings from the Old Testament, from the Epistles, and from the Gospels appointed for the daily and Sunday services throughout the year, as well as for particular feast days. The lectionary itself is a pedagogical tool. The Sunday Matins Gospel lessons, for example, are taken from the resurrection accounts to remind us that we are celebrating the Lord's resurrection.

When it comes to Old Testament readings appointed for feast days, we see how the liturgy, like the New Testament and the Fathers, interprets Scripture typologically. On feast days for the Virgin Mary, we usually read, among others, the account of the ladder Jacob dreamed of (for Mary is the ladder connecting earth and heaven), the depiction of the temple in Ezekiel 44 (for Mary is the sanctuary bearing the prince, and she is the gate which faces east and which shall remain shut). On the eve of the Feast of Pascha (Easter), we read all the stories that involve passage, or death (or near death) and resurrection—the story of the Passover, the story of the passage through the Red Sea, the story of Jonah swallowed and spat up by the whale, the story of the raising of the son of the Shunemite woman—since all of these prefigure Christ.

Through Hymns That Expound on Scriptural Themes and Readings

Many of the Church's liturgical hymns are meant to illumine scriptural accounts. In the case of feast days, such as the Feast of the Meeting of the Lord (when the infant Jesus is presented to the temple and into the hands of Simeon the Elder), the hymns draw out the patristic teachings about Christ that are gleaned from the account of St Luke (2.22–40). They instill this account with a dimension that is both poetic and theological:

> Today Simeon receives in his embrace the
>   uncircumscribed Word,
> Supreme in being, borne on high in glory upon the
>   heavenly throne . . .
> Simeon beholds thee as a babe, O Word begotten of the
>   Father before all ages . . .
>
> Now let the gate of heaven be opened:
> For God the Word, begotten timelessly of the Father,
> Has taken flesh and is born of a Virgin.
> He desires in all his goodness to call back mortal
>   nature,
> And to set it at the right hand of the Father.

The liturgical hymns often reveal the typological sense of Old Testament events:

In the Red Sea of old,
A type of the virgin bride was prefigured.
There, Moses divided the waters;
Here, Gabriel assisted in the miracle.
There, Israel crossed the sea without getting wet,
Here, the Virgin gave birth to Christ without seed.
After Israel's passage, the sea remained impassible;
After Emmanuel's birth, the virgin remained a virgin.
O ever-existing God, who appeared as man,
O Lord: have mercy on us.[16]

Singing and hearing such hymns, our understanding of Scripture is guided, illumined.

Through the Homily

Since the days of the early church, the homily has been an integral part of the liturgical gathering. The "Sacrament of the Word," as Fr Alexander Schmemann calls this portion of the liturgy, consists in the reading of Scripture, together with the homily. We say repeatedly that Scripture is not self-interpreting; its meaning isn't always self-evident. The words of Scripture do not of themselves convey holiness; they must be read in a language that is understood by the people, and they must be followed up with words that assist in their integration in the life of the community. The preacher stands in the front of the congregation; he represents the Church and its conciliar tradition, its apostolic faith. This is an immense responsibility, one which ought to reflect an immersion in the life of the Church and prayerful study of its tradition. It is

---

[16]Theotokion of Saturday (Resurrection) Vespers, Tone 5.

incumbent on this person to preach the gospel, the very same gospel that is conveyed in the Holy Scriptures.

Through the Veneration of Scripture and the Gospel Book

The Scriptures, particularly in the liturgical context, are an object of veneration for Orthodox Christians. The Gospel book, which rests at all times on the altar table, is itself an icon of Christ—sometimes bound in precious metals and jewels, and always bearing depictions of the crucifixion and resurrection of Christ—for the words within are a textual icon of Christ. This book is the centerpiece of solemn liturgical processions and (especially during the Sunday Matins service) is brought out for veneration by the people. That means we kiss it as we do icons and other objects of love and reverence. During the reading of the Gospel, everyone stands, and the bishops and other monastics remove their headgear. It is not uncommon in some churches to see people kneel, sometimes in tears, during the reading of the Holy Gospel.

Fathers

"There is a doctrine which derives its trustworthiness from the tradition of the Fathers, which says . . ."[17] Thus St Gregory of Nyssa introduces one of his teachings in a way typical of how the Fathers would preface the doctrines that they considered to be teachings of the Church. It also indicates something of the importance that anyone writing theology places on precedent; here that means the foundation laid by the Fathers. The Fathers of the Church are understood to be those who faithfully convey the gospel, preserving what was entrusted to them (the *paratheke* of 2 Tim 1.14),

[17]St Gregory of Nyssa, *On the Life of Moses* II.45.

which is none other than the apostolic faith. Many of the Church's treatises, including the definitions of some of the ecumenical councils, begin, "Following the Holy Fathers . . ." or, in the case of the Seventh Ecumenical Council, "Following the Divinely inspired teaching of our Holy Fathers and the tradition of the Catholic Church . . ." St Athanasius summed up the progression from the Lord, through the apostles, and the Fathers: "Let us look at that very tradition, teaching, and faith of the Catholic Church from the very beginning, which the Lord gave, the apostles preached, and the fathers preserved. Upon this the Church is founded."[18]

Who Are the Fathers and Mothers of the Church?

To begin with, we call many of the saints Father or Mother, whether in respect of their clerical or monastic rank in the Church or out of reverence for their guidance in our lives. We also have the technical designations of "the Fathers of the Church," "the Holy Fathers," and "the Church Fathers," referring to those persons whose teaching has been especially influential in the Church's articulation of its doctrine. These designations have never been formally defined, yet there are those people in every era who come to be known as Fathers of the Church. This is a general term to describe those persons whose teaching, whether by writing or by example, is received in love by the Church. There is no comprehensive list of who they are; even the Fathers themselves rarely refer by name to specific Fathers but very often invoke "the Fathers" as a collective authoritative voice.

We ought to pause for a moment to reflect on the concept of fatherhood. Any kind of fatherhood, whether it's biological,

[18]*Letter to Serapion* I.28.

spiritual, or ecclesiastical, must finally refer to and take its example from the fatherhood of God himself (Mt 23.9; Eph 3.14–15). St Ephrem the Syrian wrote in one of his hymns,

> People have been called "gods" but he is God of all;
> They are called "fathers," but he is the True Father;
> They are named "spirits," but that is the Living Spirit;
> The terms "father" and "son" by which they have been
>   called
> Are borrowed names that through grace have taught us
> That there is a Single True Father
> And that he has a single True Son.[19]

So there is really only one Father, our God in the Heavens; earthly fathers of any kind must strive to image his divine fatherhood. But even calling God "Father" was a radical innovation when it was introduced by Jesus Christ, and it's something we continue to do with awe, asking God at every Divine Liturgy that we might "boldly and without condemnation dare to call upon you, the Heavenly God, as 'Father.'" With this awesome example in mind, we do indeed look to certain people in our lives and in the life and history of the Church as Fathers.

The Church Fathers—it's hard not to see this as a gender-specific appellation, and *patristic* as an exclusive adjective. It's partly a matter of archaic usage, such as with the terms *man* or *brethren*, into which we have to squeeze gender inclusiveness despite their apparent specificity. The term Fathers has stuck also in part

[19]*Hymn 46 on the Faith.* See Sebastian Brock, *The Luminous Eye*, Cistercian Studies 124 (Kalamazoo, MI: Cistercian, 1992), 46f.

because of the way history was recorded, and because males—mostly monastics—did most of the theological and philosophical writing in the first nineteen centuries after Christ. But, especially when we think outside of the technical designation of Church Fathers, we do well to think and speak of the Church's "Fathers and Mothers" for, although women theologians are few in church history, they have often been crucial figures in the development of theology and spirituality. They either wrote or they were written about, known in history to have had profound influence as sisters, mothers, and teachers in their own right. That being said, there is still a great deal of work to do before we will have done justice to the role of women in the tradition and life of the Church. Saints Thekla, Catherine of Sinai, Macrina the Elder, Macrina the Younger, Nonna, Theosevia, and the Desert Mothers Theodora and Syncletica are among the host of theological and spiritual Mothers of the Church.

Since I've mentioned now some of the Mothers, let me also make a partial listing of some of the most important of the Church Fathers. The classically theological Fathers (who are also, of course, spiritual) include Ignatius of Antioch, Irenaeus of Lyons, Athanasius of Alexandria, Basil the Great, Gregory the Theologian, Gregory of Nyssa, Ambrose of Milan, Cyril of Alexandria, John Chrysostom, Maximus the Confessor, John of Damascus, Gregory Palamas, and Nicholas Cabasilas. Those often called spiritual or ascetical Fathers (who also, of course, shine with theology), include Anthony the Great and Macarius the Great of Egypt, John Climacus, Ephrem and Isaac of Syria, and Symeon the New Theologian. There are also many Desert Fathers and Mothers whose sayings are compiled in various collections, as well as the great spiritual teachers whose instruction is included in the important eighteenth-century anthology of spiritual writing known as *The Philokalia*. The Orthodox Church also draws on many other ancient writers, some canonized as saints (such as Augustine of Hippo)[20] and others not (such as Tertullian and Origen).[21]

It is impossible to overemphasize that the Fathers and Mothers were persons who were steeped in the Scriptures and in the liturgical and sacramental life of the Church. This, together with the ascetical dimension of their lives, gives them their authority and credibility; this is why their writings ring true to the mind of the Church and are given reverence. It's impossible not to notice that patristic writings are chock-full of scriptural quotations. Most contemporary editions of their works footnote these references; we see them peppered throughout. In many cases the patristic

[20]The Greek and Syriac Fathers do not show much knowledge of Augustine, so there is no serious engagement with his thought in the East in the first millennium A.D. Modern Orthodox writers tend to focus on the liabilities in Augustine's work, in particular his views on the human person and original sin. The dominance in Orthodox thought of the Cappadocian trinitarian models has further caused Augustine's writings to go largely ignored. At the same time, many Orthodox thinkers have been open to St Augustine's immense spiritual and theological depth, and his importance in Christian thought is undeniable.

[21]Tertullian is not commemorated as a saint, probably owing to his involvement with the Montanist movement late in his life. Origen is a more complex case. He died in communion with the Church, though certain of his teachings had come under fire already during his lifetime. His influence on several Orthodox Fathers, especially the Cappadocians, is immense, even as they shied away from the problematic aspects of his teaching. In the sixth century, several "Origenist" doctrines were condemned as heresies, though people today debate the extent to which they were taught in their heretical form by Origen himself.

authors were arguing with others about the proper understanding of a scriptural passage. At other times it is just plain to see that they have so entirely internalized the Scriptures that they are the first point of reference, either to illustrate a teaching or simply to use a familiar image in passing.[22]

The Fathers' liturgical life was another part of their spiritual and theological bedrock. This life has a continuity with the apostolic breaking of the bread and with our own today. The Athonite Abbot Vasileos noted, "The Fathers are liturgical persons who gather round the heavenly altar with the blessed spirits. Thus they are always contemporary and present for the faithful." The liturgy's hymns of praise about the Fathers call them "harps of the Spirit," the ones who "pour forth the sweet and refreshing honey of dogma."

Reading the Fathers

We read the writings of the Fathers with veneration. Abbot Vasileos again puts it well, saying that "in order to remain faithful to the Fathers' spirit of freedom and worthy of their spiritual nobility and freshness, [we must] approach their holy texts with the awe in which we approach and venerate their holy relics and holy icons."[23] We read because of the authority and love vested in them by the Church over generations. We read them in the knowledge that many of them suffered greatly for their proclamation of the

---

[22]It is useful to note that in the case of the Greek-speaking Fathers, the text of Old Testament Scripture was the Septuagint, which differs in some places from the English translations we commonly use. The Syriac Fathers consulted the Peshitta, once that text came into prominence in the fourth century.

[23]*Hymn of Entry*, 34.

truth: some were exiled, tortured, or killed.[24] And we read them in respect of their asceticism, the self-denial and struggle that almost inevitably characterized their lives.

We should bring to our reading of the Fathers, as with any aspect of the Church's tradition, not only our prayerful reverence but also all of the resources at our disposal—linguistic, historical, and text-critical—in order to engage them more fully and more faithfully. The academic dimension of patristic reading is indispensable, even though we know that it will not be ultimately truth bearing if it is divorced from the context of the Scriptures, the liturgy, and the prayer which nourished the patristic writings in the first place.

A genuine reading of the Fathers is also a realistic one. As Professor Serge Verhovskoy often used to say in the classroom, "The Holy Fathers are not Holy Spirits." The Fathers are human beings in history, seeking to articulate the mind of the Church. They are naturally bound by the limitations of the times and cultures from which and for which they wrote. In the case of the Greek Fathers, classical Greek philosophy and its terminology had an enormous influence on their language as well as on their categories of thinking; their training in rhetoric influenced their style of argumentation.

It also follows that, as mentioned earlier, some of the questions that interest us today did not occur to them. Let's take for example our interest in gender, sexuality, and marriage. As it happens, the most educated and authoritative writers of the first millennium of church history and beyond were, in more cases than not, celibate. That celibacy is a great gift and a high calling, one that

---

[24]Ironically, their exile and torture was often at the hands of people acting in defense of what they thought was the Church.

enables a very particular kind of focus on theology and life. It didn't forbid the Fathers from reflecting on gender and marriage, but in fact very few of them did so. We have little patristic writing that addresses the vocation of married life, the vocation of the nonmonastic single person, or the spiritual lives and upbringing of children. Such reflection is left to people of our own day who must base their thinking on what they have from Tradition. Sitting on the shoulders of giants, men and women of our time must consider these matters and, God willing, articulate opinions that may someday be recognized as teachings of the Church.

The corpus of patristic texts is not on a par with Holy Scripture. Of course, even with Scripture we shouldn't proof-text, taking brief references out of context. All the more so, then, we should not do this with the Fathers. Fr Georges Florovsky said that we must acquire a "patristic mind," which is in fact a scriptural mind. By this he meant that our task is to internalize a sense of how the Fathers thought and taught.[25] That means looking to the rest of Tradition, and perhaps in a particular way to the councils and to the liturgy, since these represent the Church's received distillation of the Fathers' teaching. They are, in effect, expressions of the essential elements of what the Fathers have to give us. They constitute that patristic material that was accepted, prayed, and canonized by the Church as true, conveying the gospel, and as *theoprepes*, or "appropriate to God."

Councils

The theme of conciliarity has loomed large in this book, particularly in this second half, which has had to do with the formation

---

[25]See especially Florovsky, *Bible, Church, Tradition.*

of doctrine and authority in the Church. By now it should be obvious that the life, structure, and doctrinal formulation of the Church are thoroughly intertwined with conciliarity. The Church is not a grouping of individuals but a communion of persons—persons whose very existence rests on relation to each other. When the Church speaks as Church, it speaks by gathering in council.

In considering the Church's ecumenical and local councils as a source of theology, it is helpful to recall the following points:

* Early on in the Church's existence, there was no such institution as "the ecumenical council" that somebody could summon at will. The earliest local councils were particular events occasioned by theological or ecclesiastical problems. The first two ecumenical councils (Nicea, A.D. 325, and Constantinople, A.D. 381) were seen as particularly definitive; subsequent councils referred to the Nicene-Constantinopolitan Creed.

* Councils are authoritative in the Church by virtue of two factors:

    1. *Their convoking and composition.* Official councils of the Church are summoned by the highest ecclesiastical (or in some cases political) authorities. Participants are those persons delegated by the Church to be the primary and accountable teaching authorities—bishops, primarily.

    2. *Their reception in the Church.* No council has authority in the Church unless it is accepted in the Church's life. In the history of the Church there

have been councils which, despite being summoned by the patriarch and featuring broad episcopal representation, the Church eventually rejected through subsequent councils.

The ecumenicity or universality of a council, therefore, rests both on the breadth of representation, from all of the churches, as well as on the universality of its reception. There is no canon stating that councils have authority over the Church. Once the Church *receives* the faith statements and canons of certain councils, it treats them as the sure ground of subsequent theological reflection, and it sings about them joyously in the liturgy.

✳ The Orthodox Church recognizes seven councils as ecumenical.[26] In their definitions of faith, these councils have identified teachings that are held in the Church as unequivocally true, as dogmatically binding. Aside from these seven, the Church also recognizes the faith positions and canons from several councils that did not have ecumenical representation. These local councils, such as the Council of Gangra (fourth century) and the Palamite councils (fourteenth century) are also

---

[26]Several churches which rejected the fifth-century council of Chalcedon are also referred to today under the name Orthodox, often preceded by the qualifier "Oriental," or "Non-Chalcedonian." These churches (Ethiopian, Coptic, Armenian, Syrian, and Indian) recognize the three ecumenical councils that preceded Chalcedon. A dialogue was initiated in the 1960s between the (Chalcedonian) Orthodox Church and the non-Chalcedonian churches. That process, which continues to this day, has testified to a profound degree of common faith and tradition between the two church families.

important and authoritative sources of Orthodox
theology.

✳ You need to read conciliar definitions, as with everything in the Church's life, in a way that accounts for
both their context as well as the timeless character of
their truth. We gain a great deal of insight into the
dogmatic truth of the conciliar definitions of faith by
considering the context from which they emerged,
which means learning about the problem to which
they offered a solution. Anyone who would seriously
study and teach the faith of the councils must also
know the languages of their composition and have an
awareness of the development of the theological terminology employed.

Canons

Canons of the Church usually arise out of councils, whether ecumenical councils or those locally convened and ecumenically
received. They can also come from the pens of particular Church
Fathers if they are, again, received by the wider Church. Canons
are often called laws or rules. Rule is a more useful term because
it recalls the definition of the Greek word *kanon*, which is "measure" or "standard." Canons describe norms that persons in the
Church ought to conform to. Canons were not meant to be binding laws of the Church, although some do take on that character.
Canons define standards and to this day serve within the Church
as crucial points of reference to help decide matters in the ecclesiastical, theological, and moral spheres.

Applying the canons today, gleaning from them the saving truths about God and his creation, is not always a simple matter. Two approaches to canon law need strenuously to be avoided.[27] One is that of the legalist, who would see all canons on the same plane of authority, to be read "according to the letter of the law" as the Church's rule book. The other is that of the anarchist, who would say that since canons are so obviously based in historical contexts, they can't possibly apply in a unilateral way today and should be marginalized or even ignored.

In response to the legalist: the corpus of canon law—the sum of all the canons ever written—is not a repository of undifferentiated rules. Canons address a wide variety of issues in a wide variety of ways. There are canons about how bishops may or may not act in each other's dioceses. There are canons against cacophonous singing in the Church. There are canons about marriage, ordination, abortion, horseback riding, and who may sit with crossed legs in the presence of a bishop. Each canon has its reason for existence and should be applied with a view to its intended function.

In response to the anarchist: few canons are so entirely bound by their context as to be irrelevant today. Together with contextual canons forbidding bishops from riding horses, there are timeless canons that forbid, for example, anyone from despising the institution of marriage on principle (seeing monasticism as the only way of the true Christian). But the point finally is not whether the canons are context-specific or timeless; rather, the responsibility is on those who apply the canons today to search out the timeless truth behind them. To find that truth, a broad

[27]See John Erickson, *The Challenge of Our Past* (Crestwood, NY: St Vladimir's Seminary Press, 1991), esp. chap. 1.

knowledge of the canonical corpus as well as of church and sec-
ular history is indispensable.

Looking to the context from which canons arose is indeed vital.
Collections of canons arranged thematically (such as *The Rudder*
or *Pedalion*) are in many ways useful but also are artificial, as they
divorce canons from the situations and times they addressed.
Attention to context alerts us to another important fact: canons
may evolve over time in response to new situations. There are
canons that supersede previous canons, not about theological
truth but, for instance, about how many bishops need to be present at an episcopal consecration, and whether a deacon may
marry after his ordination.

Considering the contextual dimension of a canon is not an excuse
to dismiss it, or canon law in general, by relativizing it away.
There is no getting around the canons. There are stricter and
looser applications of them, but that depends both on discernment of the timeless spirit behind the canon's letter, as well as discernment of the situation to which the canon is being applied. A
good spiritual guide is adept at *oikonomia*, which means "house-
hold management" or, in the case of the Church, the art of applying canons so as to promote the salvation of all concerned. Those
who apply the canons today—and it's the bishops and their des-
ignated clergy who bear a particular responsibility in this task—
must understand the disposition and needs of the people involved.
This pastoral concern is itself enshrined in canon law, as we see
from the final canon of the Council in Trullo (A.D. 692):

> It behooves those who have received from God the power
> to loose and bind, to consider the quality of the sin and

the readiness of the sinner for conversion, and to apply medicine suitable for the disease. . . . in some way or other, either by means of sternness and astringency, or by greater softness and mild medicines, to resist this sickness and exert himself for the healing of the ulcer, now examining the fruits of his repentance and wisely managing the person who is called to higher illumination. . . .[28]

The canons take their place among the *loci theologici* or sources of doctrine, written by Fathers and accepted at councils as normative principles applied in the Church. Properly read and understood, they are indispensable in helping us grasp the Church's teaching on God, Jesus, the human person, creation, the Church, everything.

Canons are not an easy read for everyone; they can seem irrelevant to many people, including Orthodox Christians. Both their style and their content seem abstruse, and we ask ourselves, How is this speaking to me about the things that really matter? Yet to some people, the canons and councils are relevant to the point of being life-changing. The theological and canonical definitions of the councils powerfully struck one Protestant theologian: when reflecting on what had changed his life, he talks of the Scriptures, as read through the Fathers: "I have been searched out and found by ancient wisdoms." And then he writes,

In 1972 . . . I read through the fourteenth volume of the *Nicene and Post-Nicene Fathers*, an unadorned report of

[28]Schaff and Wace, eds., *A Select Library of Nicene and Post-Nicene Fathers of the Christian Church*, Second Series, vol. 14, *The Seven Ecumenical Councils* (Grand Rapids, MI: Eerdmans, 1988), 408.

the definitive canons . . . of the ecumenical councils and significant regional councils . . . of the first millennium. I read the volume straight through in a few days of engrossed concentration, and have not been the same since. That reading affected literally everything I would touch as a teacher, writer, and editor for the rest of my life.[29]

Saints

In many languages the word for *saint* and *holy* is one and the same. In English, too, the word saint means "holy" or "holy one," someone recognized as being holy. Holiness, broadly understood over the centuries and across languages and cultures, means being set apart for purity, set apart for God. Of course, the whole world was created holy by God for participation in God's life. But the world, through us and with us, is fallen. This means that we now recognize particular places, people, and things as holy in this sense of being set apart from the fallen world.

The Church itself is set apart from the world. Membership in the Church entails holiness. St Paul addresses his letters sometimes "To the saints" of a particular place—because everyone in the Church is given the gift of holiness. At other times he writes "To those who are called to be saints"—because that gift is also a calling, something which we must live into. In one sense, we in the Church are saints. But this gift is also a calling: if we are truly of the Church, we must live our lives accordingly. We are all called to be holy, as God himself is holy (Lev 11.44; 1 Pet 1.16). When we fall away from that holiness, we must return to it through

[29]Thomas C. Oden, *The Rebirth of Orthodoxy: Signs of New Life in Christianity* (New York: Harper Collins, 2003), 93.

repentance and reconciliation. And so our life in the Church is most often a cycle of falling and getting up again.

There are people who do indeed live holy lives, people who, despite their sins, fulfill the calling of holiness by responding to God's work in their lives. There may be countless unrecognized saints, people who, in the leading of their perhaps unremarkable lives, simply get it right. But there are also saints who are recognized and celebrated in the Church. We may marvel at the variety of saints and sanctity that is celebrated by the Church. There are peacemaking saints and military saints (although even the military ones work for peace). There are nobles and paupers, rich and poor, ordained and lay, married and celibate, learned and illiterate. There are cheerful saints and morose ones, gregarious ones and loners, intellectuals and ignoramuses, entirely sane and quite crazy. We recognize that all of them have fulfilled God's will for them in their particular places and times with their God-given faculties, talents, and idiosyncrasies. They are holy. They remind us of what God's undistorted image may look like, and they do this specifically by pointing to Jesus Christ.

The very existence of these saints in their variety witnesses to Christ. Jesus himself showed us the way (he *is* the Way) and showed us that it's possible to live a holy life with human weaknesses, temptations, and passions. The saints continue to testify to that possibility, and all of them have their eyes on the prize himself, Jesus Christ. That's what their very lives show us and what the written accounts of their lives also show us. When we speak of the communion of the saints, we refer both to a community existing among the saints as well as to the saints' communion with us who are still living this life. The communion that we enjoy with the saints is a vital aspect of our common path toward purity, holiness, and life with God.

The saints' written lives, or *vitae*, are a particular kind of witness to holiness, a reference to Christ, and in their own way also a source of our doctrine. The "lives of the saints" are not biographies in the strict sense. Biographies, like histories, are never unbiased, but they are supposed to strive to give a balanced portrait of someone's life: the good, the bad, and the ugly. Hagiographies (the written lives of the saints) do not pretend to give "the full picture." Their goal is to edify and inspire us by presenting an undiluted example of holiness.

The "saint's life" is a literary genre that is often very stylized and, in the manner of legends, can blend history with story. It bears the marks of oral literature, the written versions of stories that had been told orally, or written texts that were meant to be read aloud. The saints certainly performed miracles, and continue to perform them. Some of the miracle stories in the *vitae*, however, function as metaphorical expressions of aspects of the saint's life. Instead of telling us, for example, that "St Ignatius bore Jesus in his heart," his *vita* will tell us that, when St Ignatius' heart was cut out after his martyrdom, the word *Jesus* was found inscribed on it in letters of gold. *Vitae* often include descriptions and details added for the sake of memorability, edification, and even entertainment. Many of the saints' lives functioned as the hero stories of their day; it's no coincidence that some *vitae* have in past decades been adapted as comic books for the spiritual education and interest of our children. Recognizing the existence of embellishment and exaggeration in the saints' lives doesn't mean that they should be dismissed as entirely fictitious accounts, nor should it inspire undue cynicism about the process of their composition. Rather it should help us to read them correctly, as childlike adults.

It may help to know that many of the details and embellishments in a classic saint's life follow patterns. It is typical, for example, to describe a martyr's death in a particular way according to particular models, based on the martyrdom of St Stephen described in Acts 7 and the second-century martyrdom of St Polycarp of Smyrna. Of course, the countless martyrdoms that have taken place over the centuries follow some familiar patterns, owing to the similarly brutal persecutions that the Church has undergone in every age. But in addition, we find references in the martyrdoms and in other *vitae* to the life of the ultimate martyr, Jesus Christ. Stories of martyrdoms may therefore feature references to the eucharistic offering (Polycarp and the sweet-smelling loaf; St Ignatius' wanting to be ground as wheat into the bread presented to the Lord), to martyrs experiencing their drowning as a baptism, and to martyrs who forgive their persecutors, "for they know not what they do." Hagiography puts a saint's life into the context in which it finds its true fulfillment: the life of Christ himself. All of the saints' lives do this in some way or other. The lives of the apostles refer to the Apostle, Christ. The lives of the prophets point to the Prophet himself. The lives of the healers refer us to the Healer. The lives of hierarchs point to the true High Priest.

The written lives of the saints are not intended as instruction manuals for life. If they were, they would probably include more of the saints' struggles with their passions and perhaps even some of their mistakes, rather than focus only on their perfection. Yet if we read them with some understanding of their function, we receive great insight into genuine Christian life and faith. We touch purity, and our own impurity is judged; we are exposed by their transparency to God and by their burning love. We are reminded of our own calling to be saints in our place and time. This is what happens both when we read saints' lives and also, more especially, when we come into contact with living saints in our own lives.

Particularly in the context of liturgy and prayer, the saints are people with whom we can experience a profound communion. They are the "great cloud of witnesses" (Heb 12.1). They act as intermediaries between us and God, and pray for us to God, whose company they already enjoy. They also stand with us; their icons in the church and in our homes remind us of their living presence. We have particular saints as our personal patrons and may have them as patrons of our families and our churches. We may have saints with whom we feel a particular kinship, owing to their example in our lives. Our tangible communion with the saints both living and departed is testimony to our faith in eternal life itself.

Icons and Art

Icons, together with other elements of church art and architecture, are a testimony of great joy, and of divine and human creativity. They testify to the goodness of the material world and to its potential for reflecting the divine. When the iconoclasts said that icon venerators were worshiping matter rather than God, St John of Damascus was able to answer in a way that instructs us about both icons and the material world. He did so by referring to the incarnation of the Son of God. He said that since God was seen in the flesh, we can depict him in matter: wood, pigment, metal. We don't worship the material itself but the Creator. "I worship the Creator of matter who became matter for my sake; who willed to take His abode in matter; who worked out my salvation through matter." He concludes, "Never will I cease honouring the matter through which my salvation was wrought!"[30]

We are made in God's image, which is to say that we ourselves are icons of God. He is the Creator of all. Our creativity is one of the ways in which we can reflect the divine and share in God's attributes. When we create anything from the material around us, we can become co-creators with God. This can pertain to anything we might create; our creativity is called to produce things that convey the very Word of God made flesh. This pertains in a particular way to the things that we create in and for the Church: icons in wood, metal, glass, or needlework, vestments, Gospel coverings, furniture, and the architecture of the church building itself.

Just as the written lives of the saints are not biographies, so icons are not realistic portraits of Christ and the saints, nor do they function as documentary photographs of feasts and events. Icons are a way of conveying the meaning of what they depict. Icons, it is frequently said, are windows into the kingdom of heaven. This may be an apt metaphor. It indicates, for one, that icons are transparent to the reality they portray. Nothing in the icon should make one's gaze stop at the icon itself: extreme colors, overly naturalistic depictions, overly emotional faces. The icon should always direct the viewer's gaze beyond itself. It is meant to show us the reality underlying the person or event, for icons depict transfigured humanity, which is what we are called to become.

[30]*First Apology against Those Who Attack Divine Images,* 16.

That is why they have also been called "theological contemplation in color."[31]

The message and meaning of the icon are in many respects available to any viewer, as is its beauty. Just gazing at a good icon is an experience tantamount to an encounter with a saint. We both see glory and also find ourselves judged. The icon's universal accessibility helps to explain its increasing popularity in the wider Christian world and beyond it. But icons also speak in a particular language. In some cases we can discern that language without any specialized knowledge. We can see the difference in message between an icon portraying the child Christ in the hieratic pose of a wise king, and one depicting him leaning over sweetly to embrace his mother, his hand around her neck. In other cases, we may need to be shown what is being expressed in the use of color and particular symbols.

When it comes to icons of feasts or other events, it is especially important to remember that they are not photographs but theology made visible. The icon of the crucified Christ isn't meant to square with what Golgotha actually looked like. Adam's skull wasn't at the foot of the historic cross, but it is placed there in many icons in order to connect the New Adam to the old one. There was no inscription of the Slavonic letters ΜΛΡБ on the true cross, as we find in some depictions (it stands for the phrase "the place of the skull has become paradise"). More obvious, in Orthodox iconographic depictions, Christ does not hang in agony as he does in Grunewald's sixteenth-century painting. His limbs are

[31]*Theological Contemplation in Color* is the title of the groundbreaking 1915 study by E. N. Troubetzkoy, available in English as *Icons: Theology in Color* (Crestwood, NY: St Vladimir's Seminary Press, 1973).

arranged in the form of a cross, seeming to defy gravity. He is lifeless but not pathetic. This is meant to show us that he was in control; his death was voluntary, and it brings victory. In such icons, the details are there to enrich our contemplation of the limitlessly profound, world-changing, and multidimensional event that took place on the cross.

Here is another theological message more universally embedded in iconography: when we look at any icon of Jesus Christ, whether as a baby, a child, or an adult, whether he is teaching, riding the donkey, transfigured on the mountain, or on the cross itself, his halo, or nimbus, is inscribed with a cross. It's there even in certain depictions of Old Testament revelations of God, such as at the burning bush, which are revelations of Christ. The cross, therefore, is shown to be an eternal reality, identified with Christ across all time. This cross in his halo is always inscribed with the Greek words *ho on*, which means "the one who is," referring to God's identity as given to Moses, "I AM." Christ, the eternal Son of the Father, shares with the Father his divine nature; he exists in and of himself, entirely noncontingent. This shows too that his most exalted divine being is revealed through the element that shows his most extreme humility: the cross. "When you have lifted up the Son of Man, you will know that 'I AM'" (Jn 8.28; see also Phil 2.8–9).

Conclusion

We ought to ask, Why are these particular sources—Scripture, the liturgy, the Fathers, councils, canons, saints, and icons—singled out as the raw material from which we may discern the Church's teachings? In fact, the Church does not strictly limit us to these sources. As St Isaac said in the little quote that begins this chapter, we learn something from "experience itself," namely the experience of our relationship with God, with each other, and with creation. The Fathers put great stock in what they called *physike theoria* (contemplation of the created world), since they believed that the world is an epiphany of God himself. We've already looked to Romans 1.20 to see that God's "invisible nature, namely, his eternal power and deity, has been clearly perceived in the things that have been made." We see, too, from the Wisdom of Solomon 13.1–7 that the contemplation of visible creation, which can be so very beautiful, is capable of leading to the contemplation of the Creator, whose beauty is beyond even what we can imagine.

Yet not everyone who meditates on the created world discovers God and his truth. We need guidance. And so we do give particular privilege, or trust, to particular sources. The Bible, of course, takes the lead. If we didn't believe the Bible to be God's inspired word, we wouldn't believe in Jesus Christ, who *is* our faith, for it is the scriptural Christ in whom we believe. But what has been clear to Christians since the very beginning is that the reading of Scripture, too, requires guidance. From that point, it's a matter of identifying the persons and councils who read it in such a way as to show us how the Scriptures reveal Jesus Christ and incarnate the Word into us.

There is no escape from the circularity of the "hermeneutic problem," the need to properly interpret what we are reading. Every one of the written, ritual, and artistic sources that we identify as authoritative has the potential to yield multiple meanings. But if we look a little closer at the divisions within Christendom, we see that, among the thousands of denominations, the vast majority of divisions occurred over how Scripture is read. Each church or sect has its particular hermeneutical tradition; we Orthodox identify ours as the continuity of the apostolic tradition and the apostolic succession stretching from the apostolic age through the Fathers, the councils, and the liturgy to the present day.

We are not alone in doing so. And among the others who do, we find a degree of cohesiveness in the face of a splintered Christendom. Among those Christians who subscribe to the authority of the Fathers, the ecumenical councils, the creeds, and even basic liturgical texts, the divisions may in places still be sharp, but they are not numerous. This is because their reading of Scripture is guided by the same reliable, time-tested witnesses. The Orthodox and non-Chalcedonian churches, the Roman Catholic Church, and the traditional circles within the Anglican and some Protestant churches are founded on an obedience to the patristic and conciliar reading of Scripture. Once that consensus is abandoned, the divisions become innumerable.

Having said that, we must return yet again to our basic point: all of the sources, even the ones that are rightly reading Scripture, themselves need to be read rightly. As we've looked at each category, we've noticed a pattern. In all of the sources, we have to point to (1) what the category consists of, (2) how it relates to the other sources, and (3) what the texts actually mean in view of their linguistic, cultural, and ecclesiastical contexts. Within all of this, there's certainly room for disagreement; one needn't look all that far on the Internet to see some of the intra-Orthodox discussions and arguments. But these shouldn't obscure the profound unity and integrity that holds Orthodoxy together in all of its diversity. For thanks be to God, within the Orthodox Church, even as we may discuss the meaning and application of various issues, we are spared debates about whether Mary was really a virgin, whether Christ is truly divine, whether he is really risen from the dead. Our debates are largely over things that have little to do with what really saves us. But when we do debate, or when we seek true teaching on new questions that arise in our day, we know exactly where to look.

conclusion
DOGMA, DOGMAS, AND DOGMATICS

Dogmas

I began this book speaking about dogma. I suggested that the key to understanding dogma is to see it as the Israelites saw the law: as sweeter than honey and more precious than gold, greatly to be desired because it describes reality as created by God. It's something we want to know and understand if we seek to be grounded in the truth of things and if we want to be in harmony with the divine Creator of all.

Dogmas, the word in plural, indicates the individual authoritative teachings of the Church, and *dogma* also describes them as a whole, much as you might speak of Plato's work in general as expressed in his specific works. So dogmas are expressions of dogma.

However, if dogma is defined as "God's truth," and if dogmas are expressions of dogma, it means that when we call a teaching "a dogma" or say that it's "a dogmatic teaching," we are declaring our belief that it is absolutely true, and that it is decisive for our salvation. The truth-bearing character of dogmatic teachings is both absolute and particular. It is absolute in that it's not only true for Christians; it's true for everyone. Yet it is particular in that Christian dogma is by and primarily for members of the Church. To illustrate: Jesus Christ is of the same divinity as God the Father and also of the same humanity as all human beings. This is a dogma about the man Jesus of Nazareth, who existed in human history in the first century of our era. It's about who he was and is, and about what he was and is, in absolute fact. He isn't both divine and human simply for us Christians; he is simply divine and human.

But there is also a particular character to dogmas, such as the one just outlined about Jesus: their significance has a specific bearing on members of the Church. We in the Church are meant to ground our lives in this teaching; we proclaim it confidently, celebrate it liturgically, partake of it sacramentally, and place our hope on it entirely. Furthermore, these teachings are particular to the Church in that they emanate from within it and are intended to be preached within it. *Kerygma*, if you'll remember from chapter 1, is the Church's preaching to those outside it.[1]

[1]The classic *locus* of this distinction can be found in St Basil the Great's treatise *On the Holy Spirit* (§27), in which he defines dogmas as those teachings and traditions within the Church's life that come primarily through oral tradition rather than through an identifiable written source, teachings and traditions such as triple immersion at baptism, making the sign of the cross, and facing east during prayer. While the distinction between dogma as inward and *kerygma* as outward has endured over the centuries, the definition of dogmas as the orally transmitted or tacit teachings of the Church seems unique to St Basil.

Dogmas are also particular to the Church in that they are authoritative and binding only within it. They define church membership. There are many nondogmatic teachings about which Christians can argue and still remain in the Church. For example, a believer can follow the Gregorian calendar or the Julian calendar.[2] Whether or not a believer holds that iconographic depictions of God the Father are permissible, he or she can still remain in communion with the Church. But an Orthodox believer cannot stand in clear opposition to a dogmatic teaching of the Church and be in the Church or of the Church. If I were to deliberately believe and teach that Jesus Christ was nothing more than an exceptionally good man who had an exceptionally close connection with God, I would put myself outside the Church. I would not simply be breaking a binding rule but placing myself outside the *communion of faith* that is the Church.

It is important, then, to distinguish among the teachings that are found within the life of the Church. Not everything that is taught by someone in the Church is dogmatically binding. Not everything that we read in one or another of the Church Fathers' writings is a dogma. Nor is every rule described in Scripture dogmatic. There are many teachings or doctrines in the Church; far from all of them

---

[2]This is not even a teaching as such, although one can make theological arguments for the use of different calendars. As a point of fact, the Orthodox Church today embraces the use of both calendars by the various local churches, which we may interpret as showing that the keeping of different calendars is not a matter of dogmatic absolutism. Reflecting on the different dates for the fasting preparation and celebration of the Lord's resurrection in his day, St Irenaeus of Lyons (2nd c.) remarked, "The difference in practice confirms the unity of faith" (*Epistle to Victor*, preserved in Eusebius' *Ecclesiastical History,* V, 24).

are official dogmas. What we have seen is that teachings are dogmatic when they are shown to have been clearly defined—usually by an ecumenical council—and have been universally accepted by all the Churches that recognize themselves as Orthodox. Thus we can say that wherever we find something that is taught clearly and consistently within the Church's authoritative sources—Scripture, the Fathers, the liturgy, the councils, their canons, and the icons—it can be said to be dogma. As seen in the last chapter, it is vital that we draw from the whole of the Church's tradition to distinguish between teachings that are binding and those that are not.

St Paul sets an example for us of the necessity of discerning among various Christian teachings. In 1 Corinthians he sets out his understanding of marriage. Some of the things he says about marriage are "by way of concession, not command" (7.6) since he realizes that there needs to be some distinction between strict application of the law and what weak human beings are realistically capable of. There is one rule that he makes, specifying that it is not just his opinion but the Lord's teaching (7.10); even here, he makes a provision for those who are unable to carry it out (v. 11). But Paul is clear—"*I* say, not the Lord" (7.12; 7.25)—that other teachings or advice in that letter are just his own opinion and, as such, of no binding authority.

Similar distinctions are made among other teachings; the Church even categorizes different teachings. A *theologoumenon* could be considered "pre-dogma" undergoing its beta test: it is an opinion that the Church may or may not in due course affirm as dogmatic. The Fathers never put forward their own opinions as binding; rather they saw it as their responsibility to show how a given teaching was indeed scriptural and of the Church. When they opposed wrong teachings, they were adamant about it. But they didn't hesitate periodically to set out their own ideas, which, emanating from their being steeped in Scripture and from their firm establishment in the spiritual life of the Church, carried a genuine authority. And at still other times we find them putting forward opinions and trying them out, such as where St Gregory of Nyssa is seen trying out his ideas about humanity and gender, "as an exercise."[3] It is incumbent on us to read, digest, and evaluate such opinions and teachings within the framework of the clearly received dogmatic teaching of the Church.

This responsibility for discerning right teachings from wrong, dogmatic teachings from nondogmatic, lies with everyone in the Church. We aren't meant to passively accept what we are told, but to learn enough to understand what we are hearing and judge its truth. This is exactly what the Fathers have taught us. Look at how St Basil the Great ends his treatise *On the Holy Spirit*. After going on, chapter after chapter, offering scripturally based and authoritative reasoning on the Holy Spirit's procession from God the Father and on the Spirit's true personhood and real divinity, he closes with a remarkable statement that breathes both humility and authority, with a spirit of invitation and mutuality in the responsibility for discerning truth by the Holy Spirit:

> If you find what I have said satisfactory, let this make an
> end to our discussion of these matters. If you think any
> point requires further elucidation, do not hesitate to pur-
> sue the investigation with diligence, and to add your
> information by putting any uncontroversial question.

[3]See *On the Making of Humanity* 16.xv.

Either through me or through others the Lord will grant full explanation on matters that have yet to be made clear, according to the knowledge supplied to the worthy by the Holy Spirit.

A List of Dogmas?

So some church teachings are dogmas, and some are not. As I've mentioned, we take dogmas to be absolutely true in such a way that to oppose them means to stand in opposition to the Church. The question naturally, and even somewhat urgently, arises: Which ones *are* the dogmatic teachings? Can we compose a comprehensive list of them?

To the joy of many, and to the regret of some, the Orthodox Church does not have a codified list of dogmas. There is not even an "Official Orthodox Catechism," although several have attempted, at different times and in different styles, to compose one. Nonetheless we have guides. We have, as I have repeated, the ecumenical councils, whose theological definitions represent the Church's agreed conciliar (and dogmatic) teaching. More broadly, as I have also noted, the Church presents us with its tradition (especially the liturgy and the patristic writings, as these read Scripture), with clear markers as to how to discern authoritative and salvific teachings within it. Although such discernment is our common task, great responsibility falls on the Church's bishops, pastors, and teachers. We must trust that whoever is teaching us the Church's theology and life—our bishop, our priest, our seminary professor, our mother, our church-school teacher—is seeing to it that they are in council with the Church. Such persons are accountable to the whole Church for what they are teaching, and we are responsible for holding them accountable through our own prayerful understanding of the Church's tradition.

The Church's reluctance to catalogue its teachings means that believers are, in effect, invited into a relationship, one that is characterized by both freedom and responsibility. Freedom, because we're not simply following a checklist of rules but living in accordance with a vision of reality that the Church places before us. Responsibility, because it's on us to discern this vision and devote our whole lives to living according to its truth.

Discovering this responsibility, a feeling of helplessness may come over many Orthodox (or observers of the Orthodox, especially those coming from churches which are more prone to cataloguing truths, virtues, and sins). Are we engaged in some sort of shell game, looking under this or that cup for the hidden dogma, only to be told that the dogma is really under a different shell, or not there at all? No. We know where to look for the Church's foundational teachings. And if we need a list, we begin by looking (as I never tire of repeating) to the faith definitions of the ecumenical councils, paying particular attention to the first two, which gave us the Nicene-Constantinopolitan Creed (also known as "the Creed," or "Nicene Creed," or "Symbol of Faith"). The dogmas coming from the ecumenical councils could be called the Church's "source dogmas." They are the teachings about Jesus Christ, and about the Trinity. But the matter doesn't end there.

Source Dogmas and Consequent Dogmas

We must also look beyond the source dogmas to uncover what we might call the Church's "consequent dogmas," the truths that follow inexorably from the christological and trinitarian dogmas.

An important example of a consequent dogma would be Mary's virginal conception of Jesus. Her virginity is testified to in St Matthew's and St Luke's gospels, in which she is called "virgin." But the dogma of Mary's virginal conception of Jesus does not feature in a conciliar definition (other than simply as part of her title, "the Virgin Mary"). Rather it results from the dogma of the divine nature of Christ. Because we believe that Christ is the divine Son of God, that his person exists eternally, we believe that no new person came into being in the first century in Mary's womb, as happens in normal sexual reproduction. The one who came from Mary's womb is the selfsame one who is eternally begotten by God the Father.[4]

Thus the teaching about Mary's virginity stems from the Church's understanding of the scriptural teaching that Jesus is the "only-begotten Son of God." In fact, any dogmatic statement we would make about Mary ultimately stems from dogmas about Christ. Even Mary's main title, *Theotokos*, which means "she who bore God," ultimately refers to the person of Christ.

Dogmas about the Church itself are similarly derivative. The definitions of the ecumenical councils do not mention the Church, other than in that line in the Creed: "We believe in One, Holy, Catholic, and Apostolic Church." This dogmatic affirmation and its interpretation stem from dogmas about God the Father, the Son, and the Holy Spirit.

The demonstration of a consequent dogma isn't always clear-cut. In these instances we must look at all of the textual, ritual, and

---

[4]This is an explicit teaching of the fourth and sixth ecumenical councils and is regularly sung in the Church's liturgy.

iconographic materials of our tradition to try to identify a clear and consistent witness to the teaching in question. There still are cases where not all Orthodox agree on the clarity or consistency of witness; it's often interesting to see how the different sides are argued. For example, is it a dogma that the Virgin Mary was sinless? Some say yes, because the tradition consistently calls her "holy, pure, and blameless," and we echo that in the Church's hymns and prayers. But we need to ask, Is her absolute sinlessness an indispensable tenet of our faith? If we don't believe it, do we stand in opposition to the Orthodox Church? Is this genuinely a "consequent dogma," one that stems inexorably from the ecumenical councils' teachings about Christ? Is our salvation at stake in this teaching? I don't believe it is. Jesus Christ's divinity, as the Son of God, does require that Mary is virgin. But both his divinity and his humanity are surely intact whether or not Mary sinned, voluntarily or involuntarily, during the course of her life. So while there is no reason whatsoever to question Mary's purity and holiness, or even her sinlessness, and no reason to attenuate our love and praise of her, neither is there a reason to dogmatize her sinlessness.

Dogmatic Restraint

In general, in considering the dogmas of the Church, we should note an important fact: the Church's evident hesitation to dogmatize. As false teachings arise or as harmful moral practices become common in society, the Church has always had to take a clear stand, wherever and however that was possible. And yet the Church has also been consistently careful and reticent in such cases. Let's look at some examples.

First, the fourth-century Nicene Creed, the best-known conciliar definition, which we sing or recite as part of our liturgical life in the Church. Many of the teachers and theologians from the centuries following the creed's composition felt it to be so comprehensive, so complete, that no further creedal statements were required. St Basil the Great, who was anxious to heal schisms with some of the separated Christian groups in his day, adamantly insisted only on the Nicene Creed (which in his day had not yet even featured the articles on the Holy Spirit). He was willing to accept differences of doctrine even on some rather substantial issues, such as the nature of the Holy Spirit, in the confidence that matters would work themselves out. He knew that in that particular case, a rush to dogmatize would result in an unnecessary excision from the Body.

> We demand nothing more: we only offer the Nicene faith to those brethren who want to be reconciled with us, and if they agree on that, we demand that the Holy Spirit should not be named 'creature.' . . . Apart from this, I agree not to demand anything. For I am sure that after a long time of their communion with us and after their unequivocal instruction in the dogmas of faith, if anything would be necessary to be added for more clarity, the Lord will give this.[5]

This was not an isolated instance of pastoral discernment. St Basil's dear friend and fellow Cappadocian St Gregory the Theologian made the reluctance to dogmatize explicit in his *Theological Orations*. He closes the first of these orations by inviting a broad and variegated exploration of a wide variety of topics. He

[5]*Letter* 113.

says, "I will provide you with broad highways." "Speculate," he says, "about the universe, matter, the soul . . . the resurrection, the judgment." In these questions—and we may be surprised by their range and number—"to hit the mark is not useless, to miss it is not dangerous."[6] In other words, he allows for a certain leeway on such issues. But we also know that St Gregory is crystal clear on the doctrines of the Trinity and of Jesus Christ, matters that require precision without ambiguity.

If we think that this is just a Cappadocian particularity, let us also recall that the Fathers who gathered Chalcedon in A.D. 451 were deeply reluctant to produce a definition that would add to what was said in the Nicene Creed. They did so nevertheless, to prevent division in the Church over how to understand the person of Christ. While we are grateful to God that they did indeed produce a definition—one which, it needs to be said, required two more ecumenical councils to be understood properly by the Church—we can also learn something from their reluctance to do so.

Lastly, we may take note that Orthodox teachings about Mary, the Mother of God, are not only consequent to our teachings about Christ but are also few in number. We even make a point of this. One of the areas of contention between Orthodox and Roman Catholic teachings about Mary is that we Orthodox consider the Roman Church to have unnecessarily dogmatized Mary's conception and death.[7]

---

[6]*Oration* 27.x.

[7]Not only was the dogmatization unnecessary; in both cases it was based on incorrect principles. The Roman Catholic dogma of the Immaculate Conception is based on a false understanding of inherited guilt; the dogma of Mary's Assumption explicitly relies on the dogma of her immaculate conception.

Finally, in discerning dogmas, the Church asks whether our salvation is truly at stake in the matter. Is it a matter of our spiritual life and death? If not, we do not dogmatize.

Understanding and Communicating Dogmas

A word needs to be said about what we "do" with dogmas, that is, about "dogmatic theology." We have seen how we discern dogmatic teachings within the life of the Church. But we are still left with formulas, with words, usually in ancient languages, which we translate into our own. These formulas must be resurrected from the dead letter and into living spirit. We must come to understand what they mean; we must be able to explain them to each other, across linguistic and cultural lines. If we can't explain something to our nontheologically trained friends, parents, children, and coworkers, or in classrooms anywhere in the world, then we have some serious work to do, first of all within ourselves, to bring those words to life.

Generally speaking, the average person will not leap in joyous recognition at terms like *ousia, physis,* and *hypostasis,* which are central to the language of dogmatic formulations. It's not just a matter of translation. It's a matter of finding the meaning in the formulation. Consider the words *hypostasis* and *ousia.* We commonly translate *hypostasis* as "person" and *ousia* as "essence" and end up with the formula that the Holy Trinity consists in three persons who share one essence. But we need to go so much deeper than that if we are to be faithful to the Church's teaching. What did the Fathers mean by person? What did they mean by essence or nature, in speaking about Christ, or about the Father, the Son, and the Holy Spirit? Without a clearly shared terminology, the potential for misunderstanding is great. *Hypostasis, ousia, physis*, and other such words underwent a complex evolution from their use by the classical Greek philosophers. Ideas of personhood and nature have continued to evolve, sometimes radically, over time and across cultures.

We can see the terms evolve in their Christian theological use even during the fourth century. In A.D. 325, the Nicene Council formally condemned those who said that the Son and Word of God was of "another *ousia* or *hypostasis*" than that of God the Father. This is because the theologians of the council took *ousia* and *hypostasis* to be synonymous. Yet from shortly after Nicea onward, it has been a cornerstone of Christian dogma to say that the Son of God is indeed another *hypostasis* than that of God the Father. Does this violate the Nicene rule? No, because *hypostasis* had taken on a different meaning from *ousia*.

Our double task, then, is to come to a shared understanding of what the formulas mean, and then to communicate this meaning in terms comprehensible today. The first part—the understanding part—requires considerable study. It's a task to which we must bring every spiritual and intellectual resource open to us. We avail ourselves of research in the fields of history, language, and manuscript analysis, all in the context of the Church's liturgical life, in order to glean what the Fathers were actually teaching us. The communication part requires that we speak comprehensibly to each other, first making sure that we are speaking comprehensibly to ourselves!

Everything rests on this task. It is a missionary task. It is a matter of preaching the truth both to those within the Church and to those outside it. Not everyone needs to be an academic or a scholarly theologian, but everyone needs to understand what it means to confess Jesus Christ as truly divine and truly human. If, for example, someone tells us (as a dear and pious Athonite monk once suggested to me) that Jesus Christ was so heavenly that he didn't really eat and digest (because the Bible never says he "went to the bathroom"), they are very definitely wrong. They have seriously misunderstood key teachings of the Church. They need to be corrected.

The example I just gave actually isn't so much a matter of terminology as a matter of a right reading of Scripture. Nonetheless, terminological matters are critical. As I've already mentioned, some of today's church divisions have largely to do with enduring disputes over what some of the dogmatic formulations actually meant. The Ethiopian, Coptic, Armenian, Syrian, and Indian Orthodox churches all historically rejected the christological formulation of the A.D. 451 council of Chalcedon, which the (Chalcedonian) Orthodox Church recognizes as the Fourth Ecumenical Council. An extended dialogue between the Chalcedonian and non-Chalcedonian churches has recently concluded that "both families have always loyally maintained the same authentic Orthodox Christological faith, and the unbroken continuity of the apostolic tradition."[8] If this is the case, then the main problem was that the different churches understood the words of the

---

[8]Theological Dialogue between the Orthodox Church and the Oriental Orthodox Churches, Second Agreed Statement (Chambésy, Switzerland 1990), §9. The unofficial and official agreed statements are compiled together with other relevant texts in C. Chaillot and A. Belopopsky, eds., *Towards Unity: The Theological Dialogue between the Orthodox Church and the Oriental Orthodox Churches* (Geneva: Inter-Orthodox Dialogue, 1998).

---

council's formulation differently. With hindsight, and patience, these two ecclesial families have been able to peel away the linguistic, cultural, and political factors that contributed to their radically different responses to Chalcedon. While some differences need further discussion, this process testifies to the critical importance of the ongoing search for the meaning behind the words of dogmatic formulations.

Conclusions

This book's main point is that the dogmatic teachings of the Orthodox Church are true. That statement rests on the fact, pivotal for Orthodoxy, that Jesus Christ is *the* truth. Jesus is the one by whom all things were made and in whom all things hold together. When we approach or apprehend the truth about anything whatsoever, Jesus is there. He is the Logos—the sense, the reason, the grounding and unifying principle—of all that is.

This means that Orthodox belief contrasts with trends in the dominant Western society today, which tell us that nothing can be authoritatively proclaimed as true, that no faith and no text may be understood as privileged over any other. At the same time, the fundamentalist sectors of the religious world insist that there is only one literal way to read its foundational texts, that there can be no tolerance for alternate views. Orthodoxy, as "the absence of one-sidedness," steers the course between fundamentalism and relativism. Its way is one of freedom and optimism. It rests in the conviction that the human person, though fallen, is not totally depraved of his or her innate goodness but is capable of hearing God's gospel and comprehending God's truth. Understanding is never just a matter of subscribing to a list of rules; it is vital conformity to Christ as he is revealed to us. This course can some-times feel like sailing without a keel. And some, who expect of Orthodoxy a perfectly doctrinaire and monolithic faith and com-munity, are surprised or even dismayed to encounter that free-dom. But we believe that this balance is the perfect antidote to both the relativism and the fundamentalism that so plague the world today. It is recognizing and following the one who is the resurrection, the way, the truth, the door, the bread, the light, and the life of the world. To him be glory, always!

suggested further reading

Truth, Relativism, and Story

Arseniev, Nicholas. *Revelation of Life Eternal.* 1963. Crestwood, NY: St Vladimir's Seminary Press, 1982.

Breck, John. "Are the Stories of Jesus' Birth True?" Life in Christ series. January 2005. www.oca.org.

———. "Scripture: A Verbal Icon." Life in Christ series. January 2005. www.oca.org.

Freshwater, Mark Edwards. *C. S. Lewis and the Truth of Myth.* Lanham, MD: University Press of America, 1988.

Garvey, John. *Seeds of the Word: Orthodox Thinking on Other Faiths.* Crestwood, NY: St Vladimir's Seminary Press, 2005.

Louth, Andrew. *Discerning the Mystery: An Essay on the Nature of Theology.* Oxford: Oxford Univ. Press, 1983.

Tradition, the Sources, and Their Reading

Behr, John. *The Mystery of Christ: Life in Death.* Crestwood, NY: St Vladimir's Seminary Press, 2006.

Breck, John. *Scripture in Tradition: The Bible and Its Interpretation in the Orthodox Church.* Crestwood, NY: St Vladimir's Seminary Press, 2001.

Florovsky, Georges. *Bible, Church, Tradition.* Collected Works. Vol. 1. Vaduz: Büchervertriebsanstalt, 1987.

Schmemann, Alexander. *For the Life of the World: Sacraments and Orthodoxy.* 1963. Crestwood, NY: St Vladimir's Seminary Press, 2002.

Stylianopoulos, Theodore G. *The New Testament: An Orthodox Perspective.* Vol. 1, *Scripture, Tradition, Hermeneutics* (Brookline, MA: Holy Cross, 1997).

Vasileos, Archimandrite. *Hymn of Entry: Liturgy and Life in the Orthodox Church.* Crestwood, NY: St Vladimir's Seminary Press, 1984.

Ware, Kallistos. "Tradition and Traditions." In N. Lossky et al., eds. *The Dictionary of the Ecumenical Movement.* Geneva: World Council of Churches, 2003.

Contemporary Questions in Ethics, Gender, and Ministry

Breck, John, and Lyn Breck. *Stages on Life's Way: Orthodox Thinking on Bioethics.* Foundations, vol. 1. Crestwood, NY: St Vladimir's Seminary Press, 2005.

Harrison, Nonna Verna. "Gender, Generation and Virginity in Cappadocian Theology." *Journal of Theological Studies* (New Series) 47 (1996): 38–68.

————. "Women, Human Identity and the Image of God: Antiochene Interpretations." *Journal of Early Christian Studies* 9 (2001): 205–49.

Hopko, Thomas, ed. *Women and the Priesthood.* Rev. ed. Crestwood, NY: St Vladimir's Seminary Press, 1999.

Yannaras, Christos. *The Freedom of Morality.* Translated from the Greek by Elizabeth Brière. Crestwood, NY: St Vladimir's Seminary Press, 1984.